The Munt shore

Roseman ... i e

17

3

The Keelies

St Catherine's Place

East Rd (Eastie)

12

Hospital

Eastbank

The Willows

Willow Burn

Berstane Rd

14

Easthill Quarries

'The Shore'
and roond aboot

Growing up in wartime Kirkwall

Written and Illustrated by Dave Tinch

2003
The Orcadian Limited (Kirkwall Press)

For Karen, Hollie and Oliver

Contents . . .

Published by The Orcadian Limited (Kirkwall Press)
Hell's Half Acre, Hatston, Kirkwall, Orkney, Scotland, KW15 1DW
Tel. 01856 879000 • Fax 01856 879001 • www.orcadian.co.uk

ISBN 1-902957-20-2

Printed by The Orcadian Limited

List of paintings . . .

Sleepy old town i

The Strynd - looking down vi

Albert Street - 'Daddy Ivy's' on right viii

Lone sandpiper x

Westerly Gale x

Treblo xii

Moonlit breaker xiii

The Shore xiv

Shore Street - the way it was 2

The Corny 3

Harbour Street 4

Bridge Street 5

The Brig 6

Albert Street - lower end 7

Albert Street - the big tree 8

Broad Street 9

Victoria Street 11

Victoria Street - 'Geish's' shop on right 13

Tillywups 15

Cromarty's Lane 16

Storm clouds gather - Scapa 1939 27

War and peace - Scapa 34

The Strynd - showing K.G.S. 36

Kirkwall Grammar School 37

King Street 42

Scapa beach 52

The Willows 54

Earl's Palace 55

Happy days 57

Treasure seekers 58

Home time 58

Night at the 'sillocks' 60

Takin' spoots 61

Toast for supper 78

Balfour Village area 86

Slipway and 'loo' - Balfour Village 88

Brecks 90

Dam builders 92

Elwick 96

Stromness 99

Humphreys 100

The main street - Stromness 101

St Magnus Cathedral - interior 106

List of photographs . . .

May I offer an apology here for names missing from the photographs. The faces are still familiar, but after about 60 years the names have escaped me. Best efforts have been made, mainly by talking to contemporaries, but without success. If anyone can fill in any of the gaps I would still be delighted to get them, even if it is too late for the book.

Maps . . .

Acknowledgements . . .

There are many people to whom I would like to say a big thank you for helping with this narrative, most of them relatives and close friends; too many to mention individually, and if I tried I would be sure to miss someone out. Their contributions have mostly been given in the course of pleasant evenings spent together going over old times. They recalled things that I either did not know or had forgotten, and corrected things that time had distorted in my memory. Their contribution has been invaluable. To James Miller for his constant help and support with this project. To Pam Beasant and the various members of staff involved in the production. To Tim Foxall who proof-read the book and gave a great deal of helpful advice, most of which I have taken. To Karen Elwis, for permission to use her beautiful little poem.

Most of the credit, however, must go to my family; to two very special grandchildren, Hollie and Oliver, who involved me in various school activities and projects, which pointed out to me just how much life has changed since I was their age and which unknowingly planted the seed for what follows; to my daughter, Karen, who suggested many improvements in content and structure, who helped me to see a much more balanced view of the changes that have occurred during her lifetime than I could have produced, and who recalled many stories told to her when she was a child. To Mark, for putting up with all of us talking endlessly about things which meant nothing to him, and of which he could have had no knowledge; and last, but certainly not least, to Moyra, my wife, who has a much sharper memory than I do, who sat up many nights well into the small hours listening, while I sat with pen and notebook at hand, as we mulled over things that happened many years ago. She had the fortitude to point out where she could see I was wrong, or where she thought that things could be improved. Without her input and encouragement this book would not have been written. A huge thank you to them all, not just for helping, but also for being the best family any man could ask for.

Westerly Gale

Lone sandpiper

Prologue . . .

This is a book about Orkney, in particular Kirkwall, during the 1930s and '40s, as seen through a young person's eyes, during one of the most eventful periods of our time. Perhaps for those not acquainted with our islands, a brief introduction may be helpful.

The weather, along with the sea, are the dominating influences on life in Orkney. We hope for regular sun-drenched summers, seldom get them, but we are realistic enough to know that you don't live or visit here for the weather. It is the variety, however, that makes it interesting. We do not get 365 days of unbroken sunshine every year - who would want it? - neither are we snow-covered and icebound all year-round like some places, and we have less rain than Manchester or Glasgow. What we do have is wind, frequently, in a wide variety of strengths and directions. Every day tends to be different, which has a definite bearing on what can be done, especially for those who work outside, such as farmers, fishermen or tradesmen. Activities, at work or pleasure, are tailored to meet all of the weather's vagaries, and there is always something to do, regardless. This is usually worked out the day before, taking into account traditional weather signs.

We are brought up with sayings which mainly predict unpleasant or severe, rather than good, weather. The various phases of the moon seem to play a big part. Seeing a halo round the moon, for instance, or the new moon with the outline of the old one still visibly enclosed, are considered to be bad omens. The 'Merry Dancers' or aurora borealis, red skies in the morning, unusual calms, are all sure indicators of imminent storms. A red sky at night is a good sign. In snow-time, a quick thaw is a sure sign that snow will soon be back and a frost that is too white will not last. 'Look to the lea' was always the preferred option for likely changes in the weather. All in all, these signs are much more reliable than the national weather forecast, and in a place where it plays such a big part in people's daily routines, any guidance that helps is taken seriously.

Summer days are long, with almost 24 hours of daylight in June and July, but, to balance that, winter days are equally short and darkness prevails most of the day. With no lighting in the country districts (and, as was the case during the war, in town), on a moonless, starless night, dark is dark.

The atmosphere created by sun and rain is familiar enough anywhere in Britain, but that created by a full-blooded gale and the sea forces that go with it has to be experienced and enjoyed. A story by one of the local 'characters' of the time, telling of a gale that was so strong that one of his hens laid the same egg three times, can safely be discounted. It can get to the stage, however, when walking against it, or cycling against it, is hopeless, and running with it positively dangerous. On one particular occasion, a Kirkwall man of immense strength, while rounding a corner, was caught by the full force of a gale. He started running, and, as he could not stop, he had to pick up the wee guy in front of him and carry him bodily till he could get himself under control. This caused some considerable amusement to onlookers, but it was far from amusing to the 'passenger'.

At sea, severe weather conditions can be very dangerous, and many lives have been lost in Orkney waters; experienced sailors, lifeboatmen, as well as the foolish or unwary. Locals have learned to treat the sea with the utmost respect. Even in a lesser gale, standing on a cliff top or shore can be an exhilarating experience; leaning into the wind, shouting at the top of your voice, unheard above great thundering seas crashing in over rocks and exploding in a mass of foam and spindrift, *smooking* high up over the *craigs*. It is a great way to get things back into perspective. At the other extreme, early morning or late evening, there are the calm, hazy, almost totally silent spells that sometimes precede a storm. At such times, wandering along a beach, you are hardly aware of the variety of birdsong that surrounds you, the gentlest ripple of the sea among shingle, or the haunting notes of a foghorn, drifting in through a sea mist. You will find a peace there like you will find nowhere else. Even the smell of heather fires adds to the pleasure of a walk through the hills. Surely this has got to be better than the racket and the fume-filled air prevalent in large towns and cities, where you bump and jostle your way along pavements, wall-to-wall with people, with hand severely clamped round your wallet.

Life during the '30s and '40s was not without problems. There was comparative poverty and poor health care, with diseases like tuberculosis, polio, diphtheria and scarlet fever still not under control; the inability to travel and widen our experience; damp houses; drab, cold, classrooms and the threat of *the strap* or even the birch. There is nothing to be gained, however, from dwelling on the down side of life as our forebears had it much worse. We were not 'cleared' out of our homes with no place to go. We did not have to leave school and home, even our island, at 11 years old, to go and herd cattle in a strange place, with no company except a dog. That happened to my wife's grandmother. She had no option if she wanted food and shelter. My own grandmother had twelve of a family, in the Gatehouse at Balfour Castle on Shapinsay. As you would expect from the name of the house, there was a large archway through the centre of the building for coaches to pass through, and to get from one half of the house to the other you had to go outside. All laundry was done by hand, but no washing was to be hung in sight of the castle, so it had to be hidden among the trees until it was dry. This was all part of 'the good old days'.

For my generation, however, for our families, even for those a bit younger who will not have been told much of what it was like in years gone by, I would like to put some recollections on paper. Maybe others will follow suit, before a lot of what we experienced is forgotten for all time. It is amazing what has filtered back, partly through convivial evenings with contemporaries, but mostly with Moyra, my wife, who shared the same times, with a similar background but a different outlook, mainly because her dad was away in the war for six years. This is not my story as such, but inevitably it has to be based on personal experience. It is simply a record of what life was like for a kid who was lucky enough to grow up in Kirkwall when so much was happening, but with no concept of the stakes or the seriousness of the time. Most of what I write has nothing to do with the war, though for most of a decade it influenced almost everything around us to a greater or lesser degree. Similar stories will have been written about other places in the UK, especially those with military connections, but in many ways the situation in Orkney at that particular time was unique.

I was fortunate to have no one close directly involved in the war, and my existence was more or less free of the fear and anxiety felt by many. My father failed his army medical with a heart condition that took his life just two years after the war finished, but he served as a warden in the ARP, and was even struck by a piece of shrapnel when on duty during one of the air raids. It was different for children like Moyra, who went through the trauma of having her father go away, come home and then go away again, during a very vulnerable period in her life. She remembers many a tearful farewell, and she hardly knew him when he came home. Like kids

Treblo – Rousay – the home that Moyra's grandmother had to leave at the age of 11

elsewhere, we were all from different circumstances but shared a common environment, which dictated life, as we knew it. None of it made any lasting impact on me, or so I thought. I had not really given it much consideration until my grandson, Oliver, 'volunteered' me to give a talk to his class about life as a child when I was their age. That was the start of what follows.

The decade 1939-1949 was about as eventful, traumatic and exciting as it gets, with half the world determined to eliminate the other half - and for a time it looked as if Britain would succumb, as other countries had done, to the evil ambitions of Hitler and his military might. Orkney might have been a relatively safe place to be during this time had it not been for Scapa Flow, the major base for the British Navy during both world wars. It not only ensured our participation, but our early involvement in the action. The first British civilian casualty of the war, John Isbister, was killed by a bomb in Stenness; we were subjected to numerous heavy air raids by the Luftwaffe, with as many as 60 bombers over Orkney on one occasion; the battleship *Royal Oak* was torpedoed in Scapa Flow, with the loss of over 800 lives, and the *Iron Duke* was so badly damaged during an air raid, she had to be beached for the duration. All this happened within the first few months of hostilities. Like everywhere else in Britain, young Orcadians were being drafted into the armed forces, many of them going overseas to Europe, Africa and Burma, serving their country in every sphere of action. Some did not come back.

This is not a history of the war, or even the war in Orkney, which has been excellently preserved, particularly in the writings of the late Bill Hewison. As it did have a bearing on our lives, however, what follows may be of interest to those too young to remember any of it, or those who have never had the pleasure of visiting our islands.

Orkney is a peaceful, mainly farming, community. Family bonds are important and community spirit is strong, but with Scapa Flow in our midst, it made us a target, and Orkney was armed like a fortress - particularly after the sinking of the *Royal Oak*. The threat from the skies and from submarines had increased enormously since the First World War.

The normal population of Orkney in 1939, prior to the declaration of war, was just in excess of 22,000, but would have become less when many of our young men, and later women, were called up and posted elsewhere. To guard the fleet, however, the army protection rose rapidly to around 30,000, scattered in camps all over Orkney. Add to that the personnel at several RAF stations; almost 4,000 civilians employed on construction work; about 1,000 Italian prisoners-of-war working on the Churchill Barriers, which, when finished, closed four of the entrances to Scapa; the men who crewed the many small boats required to service the base, drifters, trawlers, fishing boats, and of course, the crews of the fleet itself, when it was in. This raised the population of Orkney by some 50,000, to over three times the usual number. Orkney was bursting at the seams, times were different, and it was within this environment that we grew up.

Moonlit breaker

The Shore . . .

It was a privilege to have been born in Kirkwall. Large cities have their own culture, as do mainland rural areas, both very different, but island life is something else again, and has more in common with life on islands in other parts of the world than it does with mainland Scotland.

The dominating factors are the weather and, of course, the sea. You see it, hear it, and even smell it, on a daily basis. Take any islander away from it and he, or she, will tell you that the thing they miss most is the sea. There are disadvantages, of course, in living in a remote community - mainly the lack of opportunity back home for young people after completing a course at college or university - but with the improvements in travel and communication, even that has diminished. Roots are still very important to 'exiled' Orcadians, but leaving Orkney no longer means losing someone. As they say in the Western Isles, 'the blood is strong'.

A poem by Karen Elwis goes:

They're going - it's for the best
Yet as they close the final door
And seek to sever ties that bind
Memories sneak out softly round the side
And follow on, unbidden, close behind.

Island life differs from city life in many ways. In a large urban area you can 'opt out', become almost invisible, and nobody seems to bother. There is nowhere to hide here, and everyone has to recognise that whatever they do is taken into account.

We lack nothing here - nothing that really matters. Certainly it is a great place to bring up a family; safe, even in the dark, caring and close. Serious crime, thankfully, is a rarity. People here are basically honest. This is exemplified in a recent story told about a craft shop in Burray, where a visitor went in, found no one there, but saw a notice to the effect that if anything was wanted, to leave the money in the tin provided. Can't see that happening in Edinburgh or Glasgow.

Kirkwall, of course, the main subject of this book, is special, though I am sure that this will be disputed by the residents of Hamnavoe (Stromness), or rural and island areas. I accept that I may be slightly biased, but only slightly.

Kirkwall has always been divided into two halves, portrayed by the Ba': our annual battle between *Uppies* and *Doonies*. For those not familiar with one of Orkney's more genteel ways, this is a game where the men born south of the Market Cross in the centre of town, the *Uppies*, try to get the ba' (a hard-packed leather ball) up to a specified 'goal', variously known as Mackinson's, or Sandison's, Corner; while those born north of the Cross, the *Doonies*, endeavour to get it down and into the harbour.

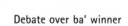

Debate over ba' winner

A victory for *the Doonies* tends to be more popular with the neutrals, if there are any, as quite a number of the players and the occasional spectator usually end up in the harbour as well. You can push, pull, run with it, smuggle it, kick it, use any method you like, as long as you get the ba' to your desired 'goal'. The game is contested between boys on Christmas and New Year's Day morning, and by men in the afternoon. There is no limit to the number of participants, and it is played in all weathers and can last for several hours; sometimes ending up in the dark. There are no rules as such, but a certain degree of fair play is expected, in order to keep injuries down as much as possible. The eventual winner, a great honour, is decided by 'debate', which sometimes involves the odd fight, even on occasions in the cold, murky waters of the harbour. Not a game for the faint-hearted. For anyone who wishes to study it in depth an excellent history, *'Uppies and Doonies'*, has been written by John Robertson.

For a time, there was a three-way division in Kirkwall, after the 'new houses' were built in the

1930s, to re-house the residents of Shore Street, still referred to as *Shoricks*, who were, and still are, a breed apart. A tightly-knit community, they lived in very cramped accommodation in houses along Shore Street, prior to their demolition. Originally, part of this area was cleared to make space for the Shell Mex oil depot, and later, during the 1960s, to widen the street, known as 'The Narrows', to accommodate the growing needs of cars and lorries. Fiercely independent, *Shoricks* would fight among themselves, but did not brook interference from outside. They also helped one another in times of hardship, and, though they were being moved to better houses, many of them had deep regrets. Getting fewer, they and their descendants are scattered all over the world now, but Ritchies, Johnstons, Sabistons, Bewses, Keldays etc, are still proud of their *Shorick* heritage.

The residents of the three 'divisions' knew their own areas best, and for us, going up past Donnie Chalmers' chip shop was a rare event. Victoria Street, Main Street and beyond was virtually unknown territory to me until I was old enough to start going to Costie's (snooker room, shop and café), and later began as a message boy to WHB Sutherland, the chemist. The various factions met at school, not always amicably it must be said, but, since there was only the KGS (Kirkwall Grammar School) for us all, we had to accept it. Much as I would like to claim to be a *Shorick*, I was born in St Catherine's Place (formerly known as Garden's Buildings), which was just on the edge of the Shore proper. This was my stamping ground, however, as it was for all the kids in that part of the town, and we are very sad to see the disappearance of so many familiar places in this area.

The Shore was basically a collection of streets, lanes, *glessies,* buildings of all shapes and sizes, a beach, plus the pier and harbour area; but to us who lived there it was the greatest place there was. We knew every nook and cranny of it and considered it our right and privilege to go wherever our fancy took us. We knew everyone at least by sight, and mostly to talk to. Someone moving away, or into the area, was rare, and created quite a bit of interest all round. After we moved to West Castle Street, however, we ventured a bit out of the area which brought the Peedie Sea into the picture, although the Shore was still the main stamping ground.

The pier has been extended, widened and altered out of all recognition. It was of particular interest to us as a playground. Every part of it had a descriptive name: the Point, the Amelia steps, the West Pier, the *Corny*, the Corner Steps, the Kirkwall Hotel steps, the Iona steps on the east side and *The Openings*. Every part of it served some

Shore Street – the way it was . . .
Entrance to the Narrows far left – Garrioch the Saddlers partly seen on right

purpose for us. *The Openings* were quite something.
Basically, they were passageways under the pier's
surface, leading to four exits, two on either side, at a
lower level. They were designed to simplify
embarkation and disembarkation of people and
livestock from smaller boats at low tide. As they were
under water most of the time, they were always
covered in green slime, floors and walls, and were as
slippery as a skating rink. After a herd of frightened
cattle had skidded and *skittered* their way one way or
the other, it is not difficult to imagine the task facing
the passengers. The first step was vital; get it wrong

Tricky landing – The Openings

and you were a 'goner'. When the Shapinsay boat was in, there were always one or two
stalwarts, such as Bunny Bruce, Jim Groat or Jock Wards there to assist, but it was still dodgy,
and many a bruised and sodden behind from the North Isles spent the day in Kirkwall. Being fit
and agile was a help, but no guarantee of a safe or dry passage. *Sillock* fishers and swimmers
also used *The Openings*, with the same potential dangers. As changes in boats and loading and
embarkation methods eventually rendered them unnecessary, they were closed off; and so
another bit of life's rich tapestry bit the dust.

There were quite a number of iron ladders attached to the side of the pier providing a means
of getting off and on small boats at any given point. Climbing up and down them was part of
our entertainment, although unless you had your dippers on and were going in for a swim, it was
a fairly pointless exercise as there was nothing to do at the bottom except to hold on for a bit
and then climb up again. We still did it.

The main attractions of the West Pier, apart from fishing and swimming, were climbing,
walking or running along the wall on the west side, or wading bare-footed around the point
during extreme low tides. The *Corny* was the main *sillock* and crab fishing area, though we fished
from every spot on the pier, the West Pier and the surrounding area. It was also where beginner
swimmers first launched themselves into the deep, and we used to gather there to meet the
Walls brothers, or other fishermen, when they returned with their catches, and bought fresh fish
from them at very reasonable prices.

Moving away from the pier, at the Kiln Corner was the *West Hoose*, a 16-to-20-seater toilet
facility for men, (not sure what the local ladies were supposed to do). It consisted of doorless
cubicles, with wooden seats suspended over a trench of
running water, which was flushed continuously by
water from *The Burn*. A similar provision was available
at the other end of the Harbour area, known, naturally,
as the *East Hoose*. A favourite practice among the lads,
handed down through the generations, was to watch
for someone to go in - who invariably went to the far
end for privacy - then light a crumpled newspaper and
drop it into the first 'toilet'. Water power did the rest.
We did not hang around long after the first volley, but
with a scorched behind and his *breeks* around his
ankles, we always had a head start. A whole new
language was learned outside these establishments.

Harbour Street was, as it still is, mainly hotels and
offices, but the stone steps at the *Girnel* were of some
interest to us.

On Shore Street, once you passed Muir's and
Ritchie's shops, Garrioch the Saddlers was an
interesting place, with the smell of real leather hitting
you as soon as you entered the door. Syd Garrioch made

The 'Corny'

anything and everything out of leather, though saddles and harnesses were the mainstay of his business at a time when horses and ponies were the principal form of power and transport in the islands. On bonnie days, Old Willie Foulis, all 20 stone of him, used to sit on guard at the door, looking just as impressive as the buildings around him.

The lower end of St Catherine's Place was known as The Narrows, and narrow it was; one car having to give way and reverse before another one could pass through. The cattle sheds at the bottom could cause a problem, and we were well-warned to avoid them in case we were suddenly confronted by a herd of excited cattle, newly shipped in from the North Isles, stampeding round the corner. We usually used the loan behind the sheds next to the oil tanks, or one of the two lanes between the remaining Shore houses, where, at worst, you were only likely to meet one stray beast.

The beginning of the 'Munt' shore took in the close known as Dunkirk. The only people I remember living there were the Foulis family. A further lane came down between what was the Egg-Packing Station and the allotments belonging to the first houses on Cromwell Road. An extension to Shore Street finished up at a ramp, which led down to the shore, passing Bill Reid's licensed store, where he kept, as an added attraction, a particularly vicious little monkey. (It ended its days at Bill's later store, in West Castle Street, after biting its own tail.)

The beach itself was hardly holiday resort standard. What wasn't buried under seaweed, stones or rocks, was covered in drains, sewage, tins, bottles, etc. Walking out as far as you could on one of the sewers that ran into the sea was a regular practice, but they were covered in slime and treacherously slippery. However, the shore itself was full of 'treasures' for young beachcombers, and it did us no harm. To us it was fabulous, particularly the old whaler, only partly decked after years on the beach, about 2 inches deep in tar and smelling as all places used as an emergency toilet smell. We 'sailed' every ocean in the world in it, hid there when in trouble, and generally used it for whatever our imagination made it. There were other boats beached there, but they were basically pleasure yachts belonging to Geordie Arthur, John Laughton and Davie Dunnet, at which we only gazed in wonder. The other area of note were the rocks at the 'Munt', a point of land named The Mount after the cannon which was placed there to guard the entrance to Kirkwall harbour. There we climbed and slid down the banks, sailed boats made of driftwood and gulls' feathers, fished, caught crabs and threw stones.

The Shore was not in the mould of an 'esplanade' or a pleasure beach. It cannot claim any great architectural heritage, even though the houses there had great character. It was very much a working area, packed with places and things of interest, and to us it was 'home'.

Harbour Street – with Corn Slip and the Girnel steps

The 'Toon' . . .

The first thing that strikes someone who has returned to Orkney after many years is the disappearance of green areas. The old Cathedral Manse, at the top of Manse Road, stood on its own. The nearest houses were on the north side of Clay Loan. There were no houses in the Quoybanks area, none at Papdale East, few out Berstane Road and nothing beyond Grainbank. Further out, there were no houses at Weyland or alongside the coastguard station, and not many beyond Eastbank hospital. In town, it is difficult now to visualise Buttquoy Park. It stretched from Dundas Crescent down to Buttquoy Place, and from the back of Brandyquoy Park to the houses on Clay Loan. Ponies grazed there, and Buttquoy House and the trees that surrounded it stood in the middle. The first area that was taken was the bit along Buttquoy Place when a WRNS camp was built in the 1940s, and then, after the war, it was converted into temporary housing before finally being replaced by permanent houses. Gradually most of the land was taken over for the large housing scheme now in place.

A walk up the main street was a different experience then. It was unlikely that you would have met or even seen a car. The only motorised vehicles might have been lorries from Gardens, Flett and Sons or Jolly's coal store, a shop van, or maybe the 'ashy cart', often referred to then as the 'shite cart', driven by Jimmy Couper or his wife Violet. Cars were a fairly rare sight. Most of them we knew, and who owned them. They were much more individual in style, and I remember the Linklater family, home on an extended visit from South Africa, who had with them a huge green Pontiac. It stood in the parking area outside Spence's paper shop, and we regularly walked round it, agog at its classy lines. We would never have considered scratching such a beautiful thing. The only car in our family at the time was a small Ford which was owned by my uncle, who was the headmaster at Dounby School. To get a run in it was a rare treat.

There were few, if any, delivery vans as such. Transport, generally, was limited, as petrol was on ration during the war, but with no one-way system in operation, army and navy vehicles did,

Bridge Street

by normal standards, cause some congestion in the street. You were much more likely to meet a horse-drawn lorry, belonging to Tammy Learmonth, Bob Bain, Peter Cromarty or 'Oxy Jock' making deliveries, or carting goods up from the pier.

Wheelbarrows were the thing. Most shops had a big barrow for collecting or delivering goods. There was also the *Scaffie* with his barrow, brush and shovel, doing his weekly round, keeping the town tidy. One, for obvious reasons, was known as 'Andro Shitey-feet'. Conscientious as he was he would be hard-put now, in this disposable age, to cope with the amount of plastic, paper, cans and bottles scattered everywhere. Bicycles were also more common, and message boys, with their specially adapted bikes, did most of the deliveries. Bikes were expected to carry huge loads of every shape and size.

There was also an old lady, Mary Ann Stove, who carried a huge shopping basket everywhere she went. I don't know what she delivered, some say it was laundry, but she was a familiar sight on the street. Andro Hirdie, with his fish barrow, was another regular on the street. He was one of our 'characters', with a pawky wit, and the many stories about Andro became part of Kirkwall's lore. One lady, who thought he was charging a bit too much for his fish, said to him: 'Andro, have you no conscience?' 'No, nothing but haddock,' he replied, with a twinkle in his eye.

Cattle in 'The Narrows' have been mentioned, but, in fact, they got everywhere in town. One even succeeded in reaching Kirkwall Airport, where it was eventually shot. It was a common sight to see one or more cows running through the street, or down a lane, with several 'mart' men, or dockers, in hot pursuit. When they did manage to corner one of them, the roles were

'The Brig'

often reversed, with the enraged beast turning on them and doing the chasing. Pedestrians became potential matadors for a time, and would try to stop the runaways, if they thought they could, but more often than not, a glance was enough to encourage a hasty retreat into the safety of a shop door, or behind a wall, especially if there were children in attendance. It is amazing that accidents did not occur more often than they did. The cattle were frightened, away from their home environment; they perhaps had had a lousy trip on the 'steamer', were being bawled at, belted with sticks, barked at by dogs, not really knowing what they were supposed to do, or where to go. In that state, it was difficult to know which end was the more dangerous. It was not surprising that they took to their heels. One look at them and we frequently did the same. Shopping could be a more 'hairy' experience then, even without vehicles parked or moving in the street.

Shopping was different. It was more frequent - it had to be as there were no fridges or freezers, and rationing limited what you could get on any one visit. Queues were often quite long. Shoppers were not supplied with plastic shopping bags. A paper carrier bag may have been offered if you were taking clothes out on *appro*, which you usually returned with the goods you did not want. Groceries were normally supplied in paper *pokes*, and you provided your own message bag. They were not so full then, either. Young mothers with prams had the earliest form of shopping trolley, but it was not all roses, as there were no shopping racks fitted underneath. Trips home were regularly punctuated by picking objects up off the street, hurled there by an exasperated child buried under a pile of groceries.

Albert Street - lower end

Bargains were rare and sales non-existent, so shopping was always done within a very tight budget. It was also more of a social event, since you knew almost everyone you met, and, with few telephones around, it was your best chance of catching up with the latest news or gossip.

The streets of Kirkwall, as far as shops and businesses go, have changed in places almost beyond recognition. Apart from the extension of the town boundaries, adding many large new housing schemes, physical changes have occurred within them, which have left huge gaps or changed areas completely. They include Garden's Square, Somerville Square, Peace's wood yard, the Albert Kinema, the power station, the gasworks, St Magnus Hall, schools, the auction mart, the Crafty, Great Western Road, Peedie Sea Road, the harbour area, and others.

Garden's Square was not a square until the front shops were burned down. Apart from a few closes, the street front was solid with shops from the pier to 'The Brig'. Peace's wood yard was a huge area, with timber stores, saw mills and offices, before it closed down and was replaced in 1960 by the present Post Office. The gasworks, opened in 1838, has been replaced by Castleyards housing scheme. The power station, a huge sheet iron building, built in the 1930s, had originally been erected during the First World War, at Caldale, as a hangar for air ships. It has been demolished and turned into a car park. Somerville Square has disappeared under the British Legion Club. The site of the auction mart, now at Hatston, has been developed as the new library. The schools currently in use are all built on green field sites, though the infant school area was a 'Wrens' camp during the war. A new school at Glaitness has been added since. Kirkwall Grammar School was converted into the new council offices in 1978. The old houses at the bottom of Palace Road were upgraded in the early 1970s. The Crafty is now a car park, and also contains the (now defunct) Phoenix Cinema, built after the Albert Kinema was destroyed by fire.

The area around the Peedie Sea has been completely transformed, from what had been the town dump, into a multi-purpose development, containing the new power station, the bus station, car parks, a boating pond, Safeways, the Co-op, St Clair's Emporium, North Eastern Farmers, Glaitness Primary School and the new 'Picky' Centre. The Kiln Corner has been completely re-vamped. Gone are the cattle sheds, the 'West Hoose', the cycle shops, etc, and now we have a new and very attractive housing development. At the other end of town, Costie's has

Albert Street – the 'big tree'

changed too, with houses being erected on what were the tennis courts and putting green. The new St Magnus Centre now occupies a site that had been a bit of an eyesore for many years. The foot of Clay Loan has been widened by removing Tom Brass's shop and the joiner shops and sheds on the south side. I have particularly fond memories of this area since I served part of my apprenticeship in one of the workshops there, with John S Flett. He was a great old man; patient, but everything had to be done right, no matter how long it took. The workshop, formerly a wheelwright's, faced up Clay Loan. It had stone walls and floor and was covered in shavings, sawdust and cobwebs. It was a happy time, but that was later.

In the main shopping areas, from the pierhead to Union Street, as far as I can recall, only five shops have remained in the hands of the same families and, more or less, continue in the same line of business. They are Scott and Miller's, Archie Kemp's, William Groundwater's, James Croy's, and William Shearer's. The biggest change is in the number of businesses that have closed altogether.

Victoria Street has been particularly badly hit. Once a thriving shopping area, which supplied the people who lived there with everything they required, it has lost over half the number of shops that were there in the 30s and 40s. Gone are Leask's, Zena Bain's, Dolcie Swanney's, Walls' grocer shop, Mair's fish shop, LAM Robertson's, SS Taylor's, Mrs Inkster's, Tom Brass's, Geish Linklater's, Hercus's watchmaker shop, Heddle's Bakery, Irvine's, Jocky Sinclair's, Dad Kemp's, and Donnie Chalmers' chip shop. Other streets have followed a similar pattern, and some of our major employers, dealing in a wide range of goods, are no longer operating as they did. Flett and Sons have gone, split up now into a collection of small retail outlets, while Garden's once very extensive shopping and wholesale complex is reduced to a wholesale bakery.

Shops looked different then. They were smaller, with no stacks of shelves or passageways in between. When you go into Safeway or the Co-op, or when on holiday into one of the superstores such as Asda or Tesco and look around at the vast array of shelving, freezers, cool cabinets, vegetable racks, etc, you realise how far shopping has changed. It is a far cry from the days when Cutt's or Geish's was the place to go for your groceries. The shopping area available was no bigger than our living room and yet they seemed to have everything we needed or

Broad Street

wanted, apart from meat, fish or alcohol. You had to ask at the counter for what you wanted and an assistant got it for you, much of it not in sight. Many things had to be weighed into a *poke* from a sack or other container.

Obviously, there is a much bigger range of goods available to shoppers, but some things have disappeared completely from the shelves, and with many of the smaller shops gone, there is less choice of where you go to get what you want. This is particularly true of the corner shops scattered round the town that sold groceries, bread, paraffin and other essentials. They offered a very personal service where, almost without exception, you were served by the owners themselves.

Chain stores are not new, however, even though some of them have changed their names. Before the war there were Hepworths, Dundee Equitable, Liptons and the Co-op, all established on the main street. Boots would have been the next to arrive, moving into the premises of Stewart and Heddle's, and it was not long before Wright's also closed leaving WHB Sutherland's as the only opposition, which it continues to be. A story that amused our childish minds was about the gentleman who went into Sutherland's and asked for a *chanty*. He was told that they had none, but maybe he should try Boots. 'I have done that', he replied, 'but it keeps coming out through the pyeholes.'

Catalogues for home shopping are also much more widespread now. At one time only JD Williams and Oxendales provided this service, and they were very popular in rural and island districts, where it was less easy to get to shops in Kirkwall or Stromness.

Several shops are worthy of a special mention because of their unique style. Robbie Milne's was basically a quality furniture shop, but he also sold musical instruments and radios, and was the agent for HMV (His Master's Voice). Originally, the shop was a long narrow building, not more than twelve or fifteen feet wide, but it seemed to go on forever, with a single passage down one side, and furniture piled down the other up to ceiling level. His new showroom, built alongside, followed the same pattern, only, as the roof was higher, he could also pile the furniture higher. Robbie himself, a very congenial, but also a very large, man, squeezed and climbed his way around the premises all day long, and always seemed to know exactly where everything was, even if buried under a mountain of stuff. No one ever came away with a sore heart, though it was possible to go in for a packet of gramophone needles and come out with a three-piece suite. As far as I can remember he only had a wheelbarrow for transport.

Flett and Sons, opened in 1871, was another shop of note; in fact, it was several shops, selling hardware, groceries, baking, bread and sweeties, and it had a large store containing seeds and fertilisers. In addition, you could get keys fitted, glass cut to size, paraffin, and many other things. Everything in the hardware department seemed to be kept in drawers or boxes piled high on shelves. My uncle Teddy was in charge of this department and he appeared to know exactly which box contained whatever was asked for. Outwith the store there were several shop vans, and a number of shop boats; *Queen of the Isles*, the *Narcissus*, and the *Mountaineer*, which served the islands. They also had a branch in Finstown. Being close to the pier, it was very handy for people from the North Isles. The company finally ceased trading in 1982.

Garden's Store, next door, which began in 1892, was also a huge employer, and was certainly the biggest shopping complex in Orkney when in full swing. One of my earliest memories is of the huge fire there. I can smell the smoke, and picture flames and sparks yet, as we lived in an upstairs flat just across the yard at the back of the main store. We watched it with some alarm, as there was a danger that it might spread to the nearby Shell Mex oil depot. Fortunately, heroic efforts by the local fire brigade, using very primitive equipment by current standards, prevented this. Before the fire there was a china shop, and also a drapery and shoe shop, all of which were destroyed. There was a comprehensive wholesale department with hardware, household goods etc, and a bakery, which supplied other shops in the town. It also contained a large seeds and fertiliser store. In addition, there were branches in Harray and Orphir, several shop vans, a boat which toured the isles, a lemonade factory, a meal mill and they employed several weavers. It truly was the 'superstore' of the time. The lemonade, or 'aerated water' factory, which was in our street, had access to natural springs. A visit there was a regular thing, and, apart from getting a free sample of the produce from Roland Barnet, the man in charge, we also got a handful of the serrated metal corks that they used, which we used for marbles when they were in short supply.

The manager of Garden's at this time was Mr John Mooney, a local man, who, by his own industry and ability had worked his way up through the firm to the top. He was a very small man in stature, and always, as I remember, dressed in a black pinstripe suit and bowler hat. He was also a very kindly and patient man, but on two occasions this was severely put to the test. The first concerned two young lads, big for their age, to whom Mr Mooney, on his way to work from his house out the Munt road, regularly gave a penny for sweets. Unfortunately, the relationship was spoiled when the lads ran to meet him one morning demanding their pennies. Mr Mooney, quite rightly, admonished them, saying it was nice to receive a gift but not to ask for it, and, as a punishment, there would be no pennies that day. 'All right Geordie,' said one, 'You ha'd the peedie b....r and I'll keek his erse,' was the ungrateful reaction. Mercifully, Geordie did not go along with the idea, but it ended that source of income.

The other occasion concerned two staff members who worked in the main store, and who were given to a bit of high jinks. On this particular day, one was carrying a pile of boxes down the open tread wooden stair, when the other reached through, caught his ankle, and sent him, boxes and all, tumbling down the last few steps. By the time he had recovered, the other was nowhere to be seen. However, on investigation, he noticed that the door of one of the roofless, toilet cubicles was locked, and, after a quick dash up to the stables at the back, he returned, and launched a shovel full of horse manure over the door. After some commotion inside, the door

Victoria Street

opened, and out strode Mr Mooney, all four foot six of him, scraping horse sh..e off the shoulders of his best jacket. Needless to say, he was not pleased, and the unfortunate lad was sacked on the spot. There was a happy ending to this tale, however, as the young man decided to take his chances in the 'New World'. He prospered, and, after some years returned on holiday, a dollar millionaire. Mr Mooney, being the kind of man he was, would have been proud of him.

Among the smaller shops, Nicol Spence's was mainly a ships' chandlers, but stocked hardware as well, and the smell of tarry rope was very distinctive when you entered. Peter Shearer's was a high class, bespoke tailor's, who also had a lucrative extra during the war as the shop where officers, when they were promoted, went to get their gold braid upgraded. Foubister's tobacco and grocery shop was one of the few shops that hardly changed at all over the years, until the last owner, Mr Sinclair, gave it up. He was unique in many ways, offering an excellent delivery service, which he himself provided on a message bike. He rarely failed to complete an order, as anything he was short of, he went and bought from another shop. That kind of service is not available now. LAM Robertson's was in fact two shops, one in Albert Street and one in Victoria Street, run by two sisters. They stocked an amazing variety of goods, including toys, haberdashery, handbags and small drapery. George Rendall's, opened during the 1920s, was another large shop on two floors, containing clothing, carpets, material and soft furnishings. *The Orkney Herald* Office was, as the name implies, the office for the local newspaper and associated printing works, which ran from 1861 until 1961. It also sold books and stationery.

Further uptown, William Shearer's has changed out of all recognition. Originally the front shop was not all that big, but they had an office, a room upstairs for wool, a house attached behind the shop, and a large two storey store beyond that. Blankets, or wool for knitting, could be had in exchange for a sheep's fleece. Richard Shearer tells the tale of a fleece being brought in and the owner being asked, 'Is that *ooo*?' 'Aye ooo,' was the reply. 'Is it a' ooo?' was the next question. 'Aye a' ooo,' was the answer. 'Is it *yow*'s ooo?' pursued the questioner. 'Aye yow's ooo,' came the reply. 'Is it a yow's ooo?' was the final question. 'Aye, a yow's ooo,' assured the customer. I gather the assistant was satisfied after that.

Now, though the range of goods has not altered too much, the house and the lane alongside have been incorporated into the shopping area, which now extends all the way back to the big store. It was, and still is, the largest shopping complex in Victoria Street, and shopping there is still as big a pleasure as it always was. Some things never change.

Aggie Petrie's was a small shop, contained in a hut in her garden, up near the Bignold Park, which stocked a wide variety of groceries, sweets etc. She did a fair bit of business with the people who lived in that part of the town, with the main shopping areas being a fair bit away. She also did a roaring trade most of the summer, catering for football crowds and people attending the County Show or other festive events held in Bignold Park. Aggie was the epitome of politeness.

The telephone exchange used to be housed down the close at the 'big tree', in a room upstairs, where it served as the hub of Orkney telecommunications from 1923 until 1952, when they moved lock, stock and barrel, to bigger premises, in what had been the ATC hut off Palace Road. By then there were ten telephonists operating at busy times, plus someone on 'enquiries', another on 'tickets', a supervisor and several engineers in attendance to keep things ticking over. It is now fully automatic and the whole system is contained in a very small room.

Butcher shops have changed greatly. The fatty smell of rinding down suet, which met you as soon as you entered, has virtually gone. You used to have to squeeze in past whole carcases of beef and pork hanging on meat hooks, tramp through sawdust, soaked in blood, before asking for what you wanted. The butcher then, with saws, knives and cleavers, cut and weighed your order. Now, when you go in, you are confronted by glass counters, cold counters and freezers, all full of a wide variety of ready-to-cook pork, lamb, beef, pies, sausages, puddings, and a whole range of other delectable goods. Butcher meat used to taste just as good, but the presentation now is much better.

Shoe shops have also changed considerably. There used to be no shoes in sight apart from what was in the window; just piles of boxes stacked on shelves up to the ceiling. A typical conversation at the shoe shop went:

'I'm looking for a pair of shoes.'

'Black or brown?'

'Black.'

'High heels or low?'

'Not too high.'

'Lacing or buckles?'

'Lacing.'

'Size?'

'Four.'

The assistant would then disappear for a time before coming back with two, or three, if you were lucky, boxes containing shoes that may have fitted the description, for you to try on. The whole system depended on a fastidious arrangement of boxes, a good memory, and the willingness of the assistant, all of which may have deteriorated after a long day of climbing and descending stepladders.

Another story concerns an elderly gentleman, obviously uncomfortable in the ladies department of one of our larger clothing establishments, who wanted to buy a dressing gown for his wife:

'I'm looking for a dressing gown for my wife.'

'Size?'

'40.'

'Hips or chest?'

'Waist,' was the defiant reply.

Victoria Street – Geish's shop on the right

'A good fit' was sometimes achieved by one particular gents' outfitter, who would reach round your back, and take a handful of the jacket you were trying on, thus making it look better from the front. There were tricks in all trades.

Appro was a big thing. There may have been a lack of changing rooms, and, anyhow, Orcadians would have been a bit reluctant to undress in a shop; so everyone expected, and got, several items of clothing, or shoes, home on approval. There were occasions when this was stretched a bit far, as in the case of an elderly neighbour, who went back with two pairs of 'wheeling' drawers that she had bought for her husband three years earlier. The old man had become ill, taken to his bed and died during this time, but 'he never hid them on'. To the credit of the shop concerned, they refunded her money in full.

Another place of note, 'Dad' Kemp's barber shop, was a *lightsome* place to go in, even as a child, where you were perched on a box on top of the barber's chair, to make things easier. He always had a dog, usually asleep on the floor somewhere. 'Dad' had the happy knack of introducing a topic that soon had all the customers chatting, while he smiled quietly and got on with his job. Also in this category was the Walls' Brothers cycle shop. They also traded in coal and motor cycles, but the bike shop was where you went to get brake blocks, punctures mended and, if you could afford it, a new Rudge Whitworth bike. Alfie senior was a gentle, good-natured soul, who had a great sense of humour, as did his nephew, 'Wassy', who took over the business. Many a happy hour was spent there, mostly telling stories.

Perhaps shops have lost some of the personal, homely and relaxed atmosphere that used to meet you as you walked in the door?

For those who wish to compare the various shops between the 1930s and 40s and the present day there is an appendix listing the changes. There may be gaps but there should be enough to illustrate the point, and it should be remembered that many premises have changed use and ownership several times over this period.

What's in a name?

This section is concerned with names in general; place names, street names and parish names, but also nicknames, family and individual. (I have to tread warily here as the origins of some of the nicknames are unknown and the persons concerned may not be too happy about them.) One thing is for sure, that for every one I can think of, local readers will be able to add another ten, and of course, many of them have disappeared from use, while a whole new batch will have come along in their place.

Islanders, and the residents of the various parishes, are collectively called names like 'Shapinsay sheep', 'Stronsay limpets', 'Sanday gruelly belkies', 'Westray auks', 'Holm hobblers' and, of course, 'Kirkwall starlings', or sometimes 'scooties'. 'Harray crabs' is odd, as this is the only parish in Orkney that does not border on the sea, (although the story goes that a Harray man came across a crab in the street and did not know what it was). 'Stromness bloody puddings' doesn't, I believe, have anything to do with the local football team of the 40s and 50s. These chants were commonly hurled at one another, without any real malice, on a North Isles day trip, a parish cup match, or other similar occasions.

A common practice in rural districts was to refer to someone by the name of the place where they came from; for example Billy o' Brecks, Jim o' Hilton, Jim o' Astley, and so on. Sometimes, it was abridged to a form of the farm name only, like a good mate of mine known as 'Hacky' from Hacquoy, who led me astray on many occasions. Another trick was to add 'ick' to the end of a name, such as Jimick, Billick, or Davick, and many females were named after a male relative, with an 'ina' on the end, like Williamina, Georgina, or Thomasina - a practice not uncommon outwith Orkney.

In Kirkwall, however, the tradition goes much further, and many families were lumped together under a collective nickname such as 'the Nuckeys', 'the Dooks', 'the Salties', 'the Mutts', etc, and it is this area that causes the problem. It did not bother most, especially if it had passed through several generations, but obviously some individuals took exception to it, and, in all honesty, many of the names had obscure origins and may not have been particularly

'Tillywups' (Copland's Lane)

complimentary. In fairness, therefore, I will leave it to the reader to ferret out their own examples, and there are plenty to choose from. I remember once listing all the families living in one particular street, using their nicknames, which was what we best knew them by, and the listener could not believe what he was hearing. I think he thought I was talking a foreign language.

Individuals are less of a problem, and though there were some who took exception to what they were called, probably with good reason, most of the guys from our area had nicknames that were used all the time. They would have thought it odd to have been called by their proper names. Without identifying individuals - they will recognise themselves, those who are still

Cromarty's Lane

around - there was 'Keaton', 'Mitto', 'Dwaddle', 'Orangie', 'Sticky', 'Beetle', 'Moosie', 'Nobber', 'Hasto', 'Dwarfie', 'Trootlick', 'Pluck', 'Toodle', 'Smike', 'Poker', 'Teeko', 'Pandar', 'Wilk', 'Stumper', 'Wassy', 'Skipper', and so on. It would be easy to list a hundred, but this is not a 'Who's Who' of Kirkwall, just an attempt to illustrate one of the eccentricities that go to make it the special place it is. For a girl or boy not to have a nickname was almost hurtful, you felt left out, even though most of them were hardly complimentary and often unkind. A cousin of mine was called 'Tippy' because he had a foot deformity, and 'Mitto' was so called because he had lost all the fingers of one hand in a mincing machine. A baker in town with large feet and an ungainly walk was known as 'Thunderin' Dawn', which was not too kind. Sometimes the only name we knew a person by was the nickname. 'Tara', 'Deedlo', 'Pluff n'Toot', 'Cockstride', 'Tisley'; some grown-ups of the period under discussion were known by no other name, first name or surname, that I ever heard. 'Pluff n'Toot' was apparently so called after the noise, he said, his fishing boat engine made when setting out to sea. The story goes on to say that the sound changed, on the way home, to 'John Tinch, John Tinch', who was the owner of the Royal Hotel at that time, which was Pluff n'Toot's favourite watering hole.

Place names often refer to the people who lived there. Some, like Copland's Lane, have had this name confirmed, though to many of our generation it is still referred to as *Tillywups.* Others, such as Cromarty's Lane, again after the resident family, and the only name it was ever called by, has had the name changed. It is now Victoria Lane, at least to some officials in Orkney Islands Council. 'Oxy Jock's' (North Ronaldsay Terrace) was so called after the man who lived there, along with his wife Maggie Magee. They lived up a ladder in the loft while the horse, or probably originally the ox, was billeted on the ground floor.

Shops and cafés came to be known after the person who owned them, or by their nicknames - 'Aggie Petrie's, 'Zena Bain's, 'Bessie Scott's, 'Bella Gray's, 'Davie Nick's', baker of the finest meringues, sugary cookies and creamy cookies in the land; 'Davie Damps'; 'Clootie Peters', a bespoke tailor in Kirkwall; 'Hammer Handles', 'Peedie Charlie's', 'Daddy Ivy's', 'Massawatts', 'Furty Bill's', 'Rognvald Gab's', 'Geish's', and so on.

Add all this to some of our streets, lanes and buildings with more unusual names, many of them gone now. There was 'The Narrows', 'Neukity Neuks', 'The Burn', 'The Munt', 'The Keelies', several of them; 'Back Road', 'Peedie Sea Road'; etc. How this all began we will never know, but it surely makes Kirkwall a town that is just a bit special. It is an odd tradition, not unique to Orkney, but we seem to have carried it to a degree of saturation not common elsewhere.

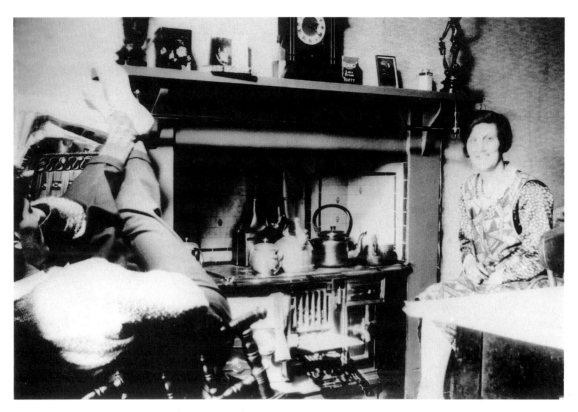

Our house in St Catherine's Place – my parents

Home . . .

Home ownership was not common. Most of us lived in council housing or in private rented accommodation. We were comfortable, but this took a lot more effort than it does today. Space was restricted for most families, which tended to be bigger and often included live-in dependent relatives. It was often necessary to take in lodgers to boost your income.

We were well enough off for space in a flat in St Catherine's Place. For a family of four we had a sitting room, a large bedroom with small closet off, and a lined and floored attic with a box room or cupboard at each end. We nearly always had a lodger or two, but at most we had to accommodate six. There were twelve flats in the scheme, six upstairs and six at ground level, plus Cutt's shop and house at the end. The upstairs flats all had an attic room as an extra. Recently, I visited a relative who now owns two of the ground floor flats, originally containing two rooms and a closet in each, but now converted into a single spacious home with a sitting room, large kitchen, two bedrooms, a bathroom, plus ample cupboard space. Though he lives in this flat on his own it would comfortably house a family of three or even four. When we lived in the street, two families occupied this space; one a family of five, and the other a family of eight. This was not uncommon and in some cases the situation must have been much worse.

One gentleman, according to a story that was told in our house, seemed to be proud that he could remember the names of all his family. When asked, he used to say, 'No bother: there's Aga, Teen, Tim, Tohn, Tally, Polly, Arthur,' which did for Agnes, Jean, Jim, John, Charlie, Polly and Arthur.

The one luxury we had was a flush toilet situated in a small cubicle between two wash houses at the bottom of the common yard, which we shared with the family across the landing. There was no bath, and the only sink was a cast iron bowl at the bottom of the attic stairs, fed by a cold tap, and, like the stairs and toilet, shared. Hot water was supplied from a tank attached to the range, which had to be filled when necessary, or more often heated up in a kettle. The rooms were large enough, and the closet off the bedroom had a window and a lift-up seat arrangement designed for a toilet bucket if required. It also had hanging space for most of our clothes. The big black range in the sitting room, which had to be black-leaded regularly, provided heat and cooking facilities, and was fitted with a brass rod for airing clothes. The amount of heat generated was controlled by a damper, and it was normal practice to stoke it up at night with wet *dross* to keep it smouldering away until morning. There was electric lighting, which, in tune with the times, fuelled a forty watt bulb, or for special occasions a sixty watt bulb, in a ceiling arrangement that pulled up and down. Lights were only used when absolutely necessary. The wireless worked off a battery.

Heating was confined to one room only, apart from some additional heat which in extreme conditions was supplied by a 'Tilley' heater. It was a paraffin heater very like a 'Tilley' lamp, but instead of a glass cover it had a copper reflector on one side to divert the heat in whatever direction was desired, and which had to be kept shiny to get the best results. It could be moved from room to room if necessary. There was also a fireplace in the bedroom but I cannot remember it ever being lit unless someone was ill. Heat was therefore a very local thing, and no one strayed far from the range on cold nights. A race for bed was normal after changing in front of the fire, and armed with a hot water bottle you dived under the covers for at least an hour before surfacing. Nobody who has not experienced it will ever know the pleasure to be had from snuggling into a hot water bottle under a pile of blankets on a frosty night. Hot water bottles during the war, when rubber was in short supply, were made of thick china or aluminium, which became very hot. They were superseded later by bed warmers; a sort of metal container with a bulb inside which, when switched on, built up a certain amount of heat generated by the bulb.

To save electricity it was not unusual to sit in semi-darkness with the light of the fire flickering round the room, especially during 'the blackout'. I remember my father whittling away by the firelight with a penknife on a piece of wood, as he often did, ending up with a small model of a spitfire. We sat and gazed into the fire looking for pictures among the glowing embers and dreamt of great things, or told ghost stories until we were nearly too scared to go to bed.

The sitting room furniture consisted of two comfortable chairs, a rocking chair, a sofa which converted into a double bed of sorts, a table which was used for baking, ironing, eating, indoor carpentry, playing games, and for many other purposes; four dining chairs, a sideboard and a built-in cupboard with sliding doors, made by my dad. My mother had a pedal driven Singer sewing machine, essential for 'make do and mend'.

The bedroom had a small, shelved cupboard in the corner, a dressing table, a chest of drawers, and two double beds, one for our parents and the other for my sister and me. She was promoted to the attic as she got older. The attic had a double bed, two trunks full of spare blankets and mothballs and a small dressing table.

All floor coverings throughout were linoleum with an additional home-made 'rag' rug in the sitting room. Ceilings were whitewashed and walls papered. I remember helping to put on wallpaper. Each roll had a protective edge about half an inch wide, which had to be trimmed off with the scissors before pasting. It was a tedious job.

The house was not particularly damp but all houses in Orkney, before the introduction of insulation, vapour barriers, damp courses and central heating, were at the mercy of a damp climate and clothes frequently had to be aired in front of the fire before wearing. Steam rose from most things, especially since modern fabrics like nylon and polyester had not yet arrived. In winter, if we had been away from the house for a day or two, hot water bottles had to be put in beds to dry them off.

Baths were less common than now. Like a lot of families our bath was a tin affair used in front of the fire, but it took a lot of water to fill it. It was seldom used, however, as we were lucky enough to be invited to use the proper bathroom facilities at Eastbank, where our friends the Firths lived. Friday night was bath night – not every Friday, I have to say - and as hot water was by necessity limited, the five kids, two of us and three of them, all piled in at the same time. Our parents also had to have a bath, and, if water was a bit short they topped up what we left with hot water. There was no bath foam, of course, not from a bottle anyhow, so one small bar of soap had a lot of area to cover. Shower gel was hardly necessary to keep our skin soft. Hair was washed with soap, any soap that was available, as shampoos, like toilet rolls, were a thing of the future. Teeth were brushed with Gibbs toothpaste; a small block of hard stuff contained in a flat tin. It never fails to amaze me what is needed nowadays to keep a person clean.

Bath night

We moved to West Castle Street when I was ten and things were different. We had the same basic accommodation, three rooms, but in addition we had an inside 'loo' with wash hand basin, which was not shared, and we also had a pantry. Like St Catherine's Place, the back yard and wash house were communal, but we had a coal shed of our own. Back yards were used mainly for drying clothes, and there was usually a rotation, mutually agreed by the tenants, for use of the 'poles', 'stretchers' and ropes. Families with small children in nappies usually got some priority. There was no grass, just an area of hard packed earth and stones but we still sat out on sunny days on a seat made by my father. We played there but football was banned after a neighbour's window was broken. Gradually, by general consent, flowerbeds were cultivated and grass seed sewn, making the area more attractive. There was a water barrel at St Catherine's Place to collect 'soft' rain water for the wash boiler, and a huge stone water tank at West Castle Street, which rarely got used for anything apart from sitting on.

I remember our first look at the new house in 1943, with its dark pink distemper on the walls, and the wooden lining on the lower part of the walls painted dark brown. It was not very appealing. The pantry was very handy and held a massive amount of stuff, including the two trunks from the previous attic. The wash house had a huge double sink with a cold tap and a 'wringer' attached for partially drying the clothes. We had progressed to a proper bath, which we did have to share, (but not at the same time), with the family above us. It was situated in a small annex off the wash house and had to be filled with a bucket from the coal-fired boiler; an operation that earned me a badly burned foot on one occasion.

On the down side we had no electricity. Gaslight was something of a novelty and it did the trick until my Dad wired the whole house for light and power. Again, we had a range and a sink, made of china this time and not shared. Like many Orkney houses the floors were gradually covered with 'army' or 'navy' linoleum acquired from service friends - great when polished for sliding on in your socks.

Accommodation was not excessive, as again we kept lodgers, which meant that I never actually slept regularly in a bed from the age of ten, until I left home to do my National Service, at the age of twenty-one. After a number of years of sharing a fold-down sofa in the sitting room with my cousin, Billy, who had come in from Shapinsay to attend KGS, I progressed to sharing a bed settee in the best room. By this time my mother, sister and another cousin, Mabel, were sharing the double bed in the bedroom.

To begin with, the furniture from St Catherine's Place, including the built-in cupboard with the sliding doors which came with us, was adequate. Improvements, however, came fairly quickly. A gas ring was added; the kitchen-cum-living room walls were distempered and 'stippled' with a sponge and the woodwork, including the dado lining, was painted pale green, again by courtesy of His Majesty's Armed Forces. Later improvements included a tiled grate in the best room, with the fireplace and mantelpiece from there replacing the range in the living room. An electric cooker was installed, and a new three-piece suite was bought from Robbie Milne, whose shop was almost next door, and who assured us that the suite was 'in moquiette and made by the original McGregor himself, who had a whisker'. Robbie also sold us a carpet square for the best room, which was laid on top of the lino leaving a brown border all round. Much later, a hot water supply was taken into the bath, by courtesy of Mr and Mrs Nicolson from CT Stewart's bakeshop next door. To get to this stage took about six years, but it was some change. This new environment meant different neighbours and friends, a different area, a new way to go to school and a lot more in the way of home comforts.

Fires were fuelled by a variety of materials: coal, which was stored in the coal shed; logs that were sent in from relatives at Balfour cottage in Shapinsay; peats occasionally, though we never had a peat bank, and coke. Coke was partly burned coal obtainable from the gasworks just across the road. It was removed from the retorts when it was no longer producing any gas but still with a lot of burning left in it. The system was that you supplied the sack, any size, filled it up yourself at the 'bing', paid one shilling and carried it home. We were lucky enough to live just across the street, and we had a very large grain sack. I was also allowed to borrow the big iron barrow to cart it home.

Bringing home the fuel

The gasworks was another interesting place to go, particularly on a cold night. The stokers who worked there were mostly friendly and quite happy to let you watch the routine of raking out the partly burnt coal, *slocking* it with cold water, clouds of steam blowing in all directions. Of course, the fires had to be topped up again and it was amazing to watch big Jock Mears, an ex-navy stoker, in full flow, hurling huge shovel-fuls of coal right into the back of the top row of furnaces. They were about head high and the door openings were small, but he never missed.

Fires, lamps, gas rings, gas cookers and, of course, cigarettes, had to be lit, and to make the matches spin out we had 'spills' made of paper or wood shavings, with which a light could be transferred from the fire to any other source required.

We had two serious problems at West Castle Street. The first was cockroaches. Before CT Stewart's bakery moved along the road to a separate building it was contained in their shop, immediately through the wall from our living room. As soon it got dark they were on the move. When we had been out for an evening our first chore was to line up at the living room door, and as soon as the light was switched on rush in, stamping like 'dervishes' in every direction trying to kill as many as we could before they scurried to safety. Someone said that a cockroach can travel at 40 miles an hour, a fact that I would not doubt. Even during the daylight if you picked up a book or a towel off the peg, or anything at floor level, one or two would fall out. They were everywhere, in amongst clothes, anywhere there was a crevice of any sort, and particularly under the moveable kerb round the fire where they accumulated in numbers. They liked warm places. Our bed in the living room was invaded on a nightly basis, if there was any part of the blankets touching the floor which there invariably was. 'Company' in bed was normal but they did not bite and did not bother us all that much. Still, we could have done without them, and amazingly they vanished overnight, thanks to the second problem that affected us; flooding.

It happened in 1953 during the tremendous storm that caused so much damage all over Orkney, with winds considerably in excess of the 125mph recorded on Costa Hill in Evie. The Ayre Road was breached by huge seas, and a mixture of salt water and rain water was forced back up the drains by heavy seas and exceptionally high tides. At first we thought we had nothing to worry about, wading about outside in 'welly' boots. However, as it got deeper and deeper, eventually going over the tops of our boots, sandbags, supplied by Kirkwall Town Council, were piled at the front door (the only back door we had was the living room window). It was all to no avail as the water filled the under-floor area through air vents, and began seeping up through the floorboards, eventually to a height of about nine inches throughout the house. We managed to get our best room carpet lifted, bedclothes up off the floor, bottom drawers out of the furniture and anything else that would damage raised to safety. We went to see how old Mrs Foubister was getting on next door, but she was in no way alarmed. All her furniture was on legs, she said, and quite safe, but as we were speaking, the *chanty* from her bedroom came floating round the door, and we all had a good laugh. It was not a laughing matter later, however, when the cleaning up had to be faced. The salt water never really dried out of the walls. Every time it rained the damp started to show again, and it was only fixed after all the walls had been 'picked' up to a height of about three feet and the plaster renewed. Unfortunately we were not insured for flooding, but at least our friends the cockroaches, who could run but couldn't swim, were gone for good.

Waiting for the tide to go out

The occasional mouse that visited was got rid of either by a trap or by putting something tempting on a tray and spreading a glue-like substance around it, to which the mice stuck. Rats were disposed of by mixing oatmeal and plaster of Paris in a saucer and placing another saucer of water alongside it. I suppose acute constipation would have been the ultimate cause of death.

New council houses, built after the war, including the stone houses in Thorfinn Street, where Moyra moved to when she was ten, had proper bathrooms, a modern fire in the sitting room and grates in both bedrooms. There was an oven attached to the living room fireplace, and a hob arrangement for a kettle that swung in over the coal fire. Hot water from the living room fireplace was piped to the bathroom and the kitchen, and all rooms were fully wired for power and light. About this time, electric and gas cookers began to become more plentiful, as did electric blankets, bedside lights and other home comforts.

Luxuries, not uncommon at this time, were a wireless, and a gramophone that had to be wound up by a handle. It played such favourites as *The Laughing Policeman*, *Saturday night at the Bu'* (with Davie Laughton and family in Deerness), and Jimmy Shand. Most houses had a card table which was in constant use for games, jigsaws, and so on. Favourite radio programmes of the time, were *The Tommy Handley Show*, *Dick Barton, Special Agent*, *Children's Hour*, *Women's Hour* and, of course, Radio Luxembourg. They had to be sacrificed when we were in Shapinsay as John Liddell or 'Granda', depending on which house we were in, did not allow that sort of rubbish to waste the battery. It was the news, or nothing.

Even though there were plenty of opportunities for employment, with gaps created when many of our young men were drafted into the armed forces, mums who did not have someone on whom they could depend to look after small children mostly stayed at home, or at best took a part-time job as a cleaner in an office or a bank. There were not many childminders around. This was the beginning of the full-time 'working mum', however, and the habit expanded after the war. They still had lots to cope with at home. There was the cooking and the baking. Since there were no washing machines or tumble dryers, washing was done by hand in the wash house with water that had to be heated in the coal-fired boiler. The worst stains were removed on a scrubbing board. Whites were boiled to make them whiter and to get rid of any 'bugs'. Then they were often laid out in the sun to bleach. Getting the worst of the water out was achieved by hand wringing or with a hand-operated wringer or a mangle. Drying was done outside on ropes or inside on a pulley or a clothes horse. The iron had to be heated, and re-heated when necessary to the right temperature, on top of the range. There were also floors to be washed and polished. Add to that dusting, darning socks and jumpers, altering hand-me-downs, knitting and sewing, polishing brass, cleaning the stairs (a duty shared among tenants), and many other chores, Mums had to work unbelievably hard just to keep on top.

Dads worked long hours as well, at least a 44-hour week over five and a half days and often much longer. Doing 'homers' in the evenings was often necessary just to earn enough to keep the family fed and clothed. Holidays were fewer. Tradesmen got one fixed 'trades week' in the summer, a day at Christmas and day at New Year. Pay for those holidays was accumulated from deductions taken from their weekly wage packet throughout the year. Any other time off was unpaid. They had no machines, power tools, dumper trucks, cranes or other labour-saving devices, so it was genuine manual labour, and workshops rarely had any form of heating.

Having live-in dependent relatives was common as there was nowhere else for them to go apart from the 'poor house'. This was a home with a number of wards with beds lined up in rows designed for those unable to care for themselves, and who had no one to look after them. Lodgers were also a necessary addition if the family income did not suffice, and visitors from the isles or from *Sooth* were always accommodated. There was little in the way of bed and breakfast accommodation, no self-catering available, and hotels were out of the question for ordinary people. There were hardly any cars or motor bikes, and though bikes were helpful, few families had one for each member. It meant long walks for some Mums to the shops.

Visitors varied enormously, of course; some were great fun but others just so-so. One visitor who fascinated us was an elderly retired sea captain from Shetland. Like most seamen he smoked the pipe, and like most pipe smokers he accumulated a residue of spittle in his mouth at regular intervals. We sat with bated breath, until 'whambo', he ejected it with the velocity of a bullet across a space of up to ten feet, to hit the back of the fire with a crack and a sizzle. He never missed, but even after lots of practice we never managed to achieve this feat of length and accuracy. Unfortunately, as he was not staying with us, we only had this particular treat for a few hours at a time, not the whole fortnight.

Punishment at home varied from family to family, and it probably has not changed all that much over the years. There was none of this, 'our kids can do no wrong' attitude. Rather than taking a supporting role, if you were in trouble outwith the home it usually resulted in getting another sorting out when you came in. Punishments included withdrawal of pocket money (which was little enough anyhow), being sent to bed early (not always practical when living rooms doubled up as bedrooms, and bedrooms as play areas), or isolation, which had the same problem unless you had an attic which served the purpose. A clip round the ear, better known as a *lugget*, was common enough, but not in our house. The occasional nip under the table, however, was a timely reminder to behave, particularly when visiting other people's houses for tea. Undoubtedly, the main 'deterrent' was the *skelped backside*, better known in some houses as the *skelped erse*, usually delivered with gusto by a harassed and frustrated Mum. It seemed to be part of a mother's remit - perhaps Dads were too heavy-handed. The 'long' walk to the closet, and the indignity of baring the posterior far outweighed the *skelping*, and after the event it usually took a long time for tempers and *erses* to cool down. On one occasion when my Dad was 'delegated' to do the business, he and I sat in the closet while he clapped his hands loudly for five minutes before we emerged. I think that had much more effect on me than any *hiding*. One parting warning by a mother to her brood who were heading for the beach was, 'Don't come back here *drooned* or you'll get a damned good *hiding*.' Strangely, it seemed to have had the desired effect as they all came home safe and sound. Perhaps it was never an ideal solution and showed a lack of something in a parent, but it was the way things were done, and if we stepped badly out of line we expected it. Nobody ever died of a *skelped erse*.

A'll gae yu something tae greet aboot

'The Bobbies' . . .

In Glasgow they are called 'the Polis', in Kirkwall they were 'the Bobbies'. There were not all that many of them, but you saw them a great deal more than you do nowadays. They were round every corner, present and visible at every occasion. They did not have cars or even motor bikes, but patrolled the town on foot all day and evening, keeping the kind of order that we expected.

They were held in awe, maybe even slightly feared by us kids, not surprisingly since they were all big guys. Bob and Charlie Craigie, Dave Allan, Tom Mainland, Sammy Bews, Jimmy Thompson, Jim Cormack and Inspector Cheyne, were all over six feet. They did not have to say much; their appearance, or the occasional *lugget*, was usually enough. If necessary, a quiet word with a parent sorted out most problems. Parents may have had a different attitude too, accepting the fact that their child may have done something wrong, rather than defending them to the hilt. 'My boy would never have done that', was not the normal view. They had been children at one time too, and accepted that their 'little dears' were perfectly capable of doing whatever it was that had caused the problem. The threat of 'the birch' was always there, of course, but it was only a threat. I never heard of anyone of my age group ever actually getting it. It was never a 'them and us' situation, as seems to be the case in so many places now.

The policemen were mostly local and were known to the people who lived in the community, and they, in turn, knew almost everyone by name. There were not so many strangers in those days, either in the police or as members of the public. They went to football matches and other events, as did most of the potential 'hooligans'. Quite a few of them played football for the local teams, and we mixed socially when they were out of uniform.

If someone was apprehended, the police knew how to make the charges stick. One guy, who was a bit of a nuisance, was picked up, as usual slightly under the influence, but he hadn't apparently committed any 'crime'. When the constable asked the sergeant what they were going to charge him with, he was told, 'resisting arrest'. The constable argued that the man had not resisted arrest, but was told firmly; 'He must have resisted arrest - put that down Wylie.' Then 'use of foul language' was added, in spite of the protests of both constable and 'prisoner'. 'He must have been using foul language - put that down Wylie.' The bloke looked to be in real trouble, with a whole list of charges set against him, but the outcome was not too serious and he was let off with a severe warning and a lot to think about.

Another tale concerned the shipping of whisky from the Highland Park Distillery. When the empty casks came back from the blenders for refilling, there was always a residue that had soaked back out of the wood left in the bottom. Certain dockers were tempted by this and usually managed to 'salvage' enough to make the day go more pleasantly. Occasionally checks were made, and on this particular day one lad was caught imbibing out of a container of some sort. Rather than give up his 'tot' he kept on drinking, while holding the policeman off with his other hand and murmuring, 'A sheep as a lamb, a sheep as a lamb', ('may as well be hung for a sheep as a lamb').

A well-known story was told about one particular constable who was apparently very 'ready with his hands'. It concerned a seaman much under the weather, who was being escorted, with some difficulty, along Junction Road. At one point, his continual floundering about sufficiently annoyed the 'man in blue' to provoke a whip at him with his hand, but another lurch just at that precise moment, caused the hand to miss its intended target. To add to the indignity they both ended up in a heap on the ground. The hand did not miss the second, or third, time.

Vandalism was not really a thing with us, although we were not lily white by any means. 'Rapitty-tap' was a familiar but annoying street game that we played, which consisted of knocking on doors or ringing doorbells and running away. It added something if you tied two doors together on opposite sides of the street, and then knocked. I have been reminded of a time when a jug of water was poured from our upstairs window on to the head of an elderly female neighbour, and when the rumpus and verbal abuse started, only a small friend, Rosie Firth, was seen standing at the window. We rode bikes down the street against the traffic; we climbed lamp posts, played football in the street and committed other minor 'crimes', but if we were caught, we stopped. Things were never allowed to escalate, so that potential vandals or criminals never got a chance to develop.

There was little need for the current ritual of 'shaking door handles', as break-ins were rare events, and when one did occur it was soon recognised as the work of one of about three 'regulars', usually correctly. Our 'criminals' were not very sophisticated, which was demonstrated when one of them broke into a garage one night during a snowstorm. The following morning the police followed his footprints all the way to his front door.

Well now – I wonder who dunnit?

During the war, being a policeman must have been a tough assignment, especially before the enrolment of 'specials', and the arrival of service police to back them up. They had a much larger, very different, and totally unknown population to keep an eye on, but they did keep order.

Getting into trouble, for us, basically involved mischief, mostly harmless rather than outright crime, and 'the Bobbies' recognised this. In truth, law and order came from the home, and there was a definite feeling of shame for parents if one of their family was 'in bother' with the police. All in all, it made for a much happier and more law-abiding community.

The War . . .

Since for those of my age it covered most of our childhood years, some space has to be set aside for the influence of the Second World War on pre-teenagers in Orkney. Memories of some of the details are a bit hazy, and certainly this is not an attempt to discuss the political or strategic implications of this time, here or anywhere else. This has been done.

The first image, for many of us, was the sudden appearance of thousands of strangers in uniform on the streets, mostly men, but later WRNS, WAAFS and ATS arrived as well. It was not long before most of the houses in Orkney had regular visitors from the various services. It worked well both ways, the troops had a haven to go to, a change of food and company from camp life and usually a generous supply of rationed foods such as butter, eggs and cheese to take home when they went on leave. On the other hand there were spin-offs for the locals as well. My father smoked nothing but navy 'tickler' tobacco. Occasionally a navy rum ration found its way into houses, particularly if there was to be a party of some kind. Some mahogany boards appeared in our shed after the driver of the Houton truck had been in for his 'cuppa'; practical things like paint or linoleum became available and we even acquired a whole crate of lovely Canadian apples at one stage. I am sure many servicemen cursed their luck, stuck in what must have seemed to the average city dweller as 'the back-of-beyond'; dark, cold, damp, windy and initially with little in the way of facilities. As time progressed many of them were happy to admit that they could have been in a worse place. Some even stayed and settled here and many friendships were kept up long after the war had ended. It was an odd day when no one popped in for a cup and a blether, and many a tear was shed when someone was posted out of Orkney. We had sailors, soldiers, airmen and 'Wrens' as regular callers. They came from Scotland, England and Wales, and included Johnny Burke, a trumpet player from Nat Ganella's band, Harry Cousins, a bus conductor from Edinburgh, Arthur Ketley, a professional upholsterer from Wales, who re-covered our dining room chairs and also entertained us with a fine Welsh tenor voice, and for a time we had Johnny Flower, alias Arnold, a deserter off the aircraft carrier *Furious*, who was picked up on Broad Street by the naval police one afternoon. There was George Day, a professional photographer, a chef, Alec Dixon, who married my aunt Dorothy, and there was

Storm clouds gather – Scapa 1939

Arthur Ashcroft from Beauly, one of the nicest guys I ever met. There were many others but their names have now gone. In time this inspired a strong feeling of community spirit and gave a sense of security to us kids. The sudden change in 1945, when hostilities ended, brought mostly joy, particularly to families with someone coming home, but tinged with some sadness too, when many new friends had to part certain in the knowledge that they would never meet again.

The bit in between was amazing. Soldiers, airmen, and sailors, especially when the fleet was in, were milling about in the street. It could have been a recipe for disaster in some ways. Nobody knew any of them, where they came from or what they were like, but the evidence seems to indicate that crime during this time was not at a high level, and we never felt threatened in any way. This was all the more remarkable considering that 'blackout' regulations were rigidly enforced during the hours of darkness, which were very long in winter. When it was dark it was really dark. Much of the time, unless there was a moon, it was virtually impossible to see your hand in front of your face. Car lights were severely dimmed and even bikes had few or no lights. Mind you, like brakes, they had never been given a high priority in Orkney. You got used to it to a degree; perhaps we developed cats' eyes and night and day we ran freely about the town.

Blackout pals

Certain areas did call for a bit of caution. One of our dares concerned the long air raid shelters constructed along most of 'The Strynd' and almost all of 'The Burn', (behind George Rendall's, now Leonards), which had been roofed over with sandbags. To run the 40 yards or so through one of them at night when it was pitch dark outside took a bit of nerve. You ran, by hell you ran, totally blind, not knowing who was there or what was going on in the place. I won't go into details as to what they were used for, but it was rarely as air raid shelters, that's for sure. The size of the 'new' population and the lack of proper toilet facilities - which I will touch on from time to time - had something to do with the fact that every air raid shelter in Kirkwall, including the school ones, smelt like a sewer.

Fights did occur, of course. There was a real old barney between sailors and soldiers at the top of Castle Street where fists, feet, even knives were in use. Chief Constable Cheyne led his men in with truncheons flying and peace was finally restored when the military and naval police arrived to back them up. We were just curious spectators.

One of my earliest recollections is of taping all the windows with gummed paper in case a bomb exploded nearby. We also made window blackouts out of cloth attached to a frame, which had to be closed as soon as darkness fell and lights were needed. One of the main duties of the ARP wardens was to check windows and tell the residents if any chink of light was to be seen, which could be visible to any German aircraft that happened to be in the area. This proved to be a wise precaution, particularly during the early months of the war when air raids were frequent and heavy, particularly over Scapa Flow. Bombs were also dropped near Kirkwall, once at Craigiefield when most of the windows were blown in. A spin-off from this and other similar incidents was the chance to add to our collection of souvenirs. Every boy had a collection of sorts: a good one consisted of shrapnel from bombs or shells; bullets, 303 or tracer; bits of aircraft that had crashed; sailors' caps, all ranks; officers' epaulettes; cap badges, available in PC Flett's if you had the cash; buttons, etc. I even had a hand grenade, completely disarmed before I got it, which stood proudly on its stand at home for many years after the war. Later additions included gas masks, hand rattles and steel helmets. Anything and everything to do with the armed forces was collectable but there were dangers, especially in taking things home that had been found on the beach. There was one occasion when an incendiary bomb exploded in a shed while being examined by two young lads. One of them, Gordon Findlayson, died and the other was badly burned.

Though there were over one hundred aircraft crashes, plus a dozen German planes shot down around Orkney during the six years of the war, souvenirs from aircraft were rare, as we were not normally allowed anywhere near, especially if there had been fatalities. I did manage to acquire a piece off a Liberator that crashed up at Walliwall in which 12 died; only the pilot survived after baling out. A Hurricane crashed in the Peedie Sea killing the pilot but it was too far out to get near. A Gladiator crashed in Kirkwall Bay, and in spite of the best efforts of Bob Craigie, the duty policeman, we managed to see the dead pilot being taken ashore at the Corn Slip. A Spitfire crash-landed just below Weyland Farm, near where we were playing, and although we were first on the scene we were chased away by the pilot who climbed out unhurt. All this was becoming normality for us, nothing too unusual, just something interesting to talk about at home and at school.

In time we got to recognise all the different aircraft stationed in Orkney - Spitfires, Hurricanes, Skuas, Gladiators, Swordfish, Martlets, etc. We liked to try our hand at drawing them, something that Roy Thompson was particularly good at. We also got to recognise the peculiar up and down drone of German aircraft when they were overhead. Spitfires and Hurricanes were the glamorous favourites and it was a great thrill watching them go through their paces. We also knew most of the bigger warships by name; *Repulse, Rodney, Hood, Illustrious, Furious, Prince of Wales, George V*, and so on, and got to know

Wartime visitors - Self, Marie and friend

crew members on many of them. Many homes sported large wall charts illustrating the entire British Fleet all laid out in rows. We had our favourite ships, the *Hood* being high on most lists, and when she was sunk it left us with a strong feeling of personal loss. Moyra, who was a very small girl at the time, remembers an officer from the *Hood* speaking to her in Peter Shearer's shop where her mum worked. She was colouring her nails with crayons, and seeing this he promised to take some nail varnish in to her on his next visit, but of course he never came back.

We also got the chance to board many of the ships on open days, especially after the pressure on Scapa had eased. It is difficult to remember how many or which ones we were on, but they were great days. We climbed stairs and ladders, boring through every hole and corner that we were allowed to, plus some we weren't and were chased out by a sailor on duty. We gazed up at the massive guns and were even allowed in close enough to see sailors operating the controls,

More wartime friends - after a trip to Scapa
Self; Ellen Anderson; Arthur Ashcroft (drove Houton truck); sister Margaret; Johnny Arnold or 'Flower' (deserter from H*MS Furious* - picked up on Broad Street by naval police); cousin Mabel. Photo taken by George Day also off the *Furious*

and we got to see the huge engines. It was always with reluctance that we had to take our place on one of the launches back to Scapa Pier. There were also visits to smaller vessels at Kirkwall Pier - a submarine on one occasion, and HMS *Ness*, a frigate built with money raised by the people of Orkney during one of the many money raising weeks held at this time. Spitfire Week, Wings for Victory Week, War Weapons Week, Salute the Soldier Week and similar events took place at regular intervals. Each time a large pole was erected on Broad Street with markings on it like a thermometer to indicate how the money collected was rising. These occasions were usually supported by displays on the Market Green of something of a military nature.

Transport had to be provided to cart the thousands of naval personnel back and fore between Kirkwall and Scapa Pier, where tenders ferried them to and from their ships. The main bus involved in this, as well as meeting the regular passenger ferry from Scrabster, was driven by Bob Slater. In fact it was just called Bob Slater's bus even though it was one of John G Nicolson's fleet. Bob was a very likeable, round man with a jovial Harry Secombe-type face that was always cheery, always beaming. It must have been a tough assignment carting drunk or half-drunk sailors back to Scapa after a night in the town. The bus was always packed to capacity, with more standing than sitting, but he took it all in his stride. On one occasion, however, a group of sailors had decided they were not going to pay the few pence fare. The leader, a big English lad, took the initiative threatening, 'You'll not be getting any fares tonight and I'd better warn you before you try anything stupid, I am the heavy-weight champion of the British navy.' Bob quietly leaned inside the bus door, picked up the *wap* and clobbered him over the head, dropping him on the pier like a stone, completely out for the count. 'Next champ please,' Bob invited. There were no takers, all paid without a murmur and after the word got round he had no further trouble. Incidentally, Bob was also the driver on the day that the new Chief Constable and his wife arrived on the ferry. Being a cold day Bob was sensibly wearing a balaclava. Coming from Glasgow, the lady concerned must have had some pre-conceived ideas of what Orkney would be like, for on sighting Bob's cheery face peering out from under the brim of his balaclava she exclaimed, 'Oh ma Loard; Eskimos.'

We also had many important visitors, which meant little to us. I remember sitting on top of a bus near Kirkwall pier watching King George VI go past, but we never saw, nor were we too concerned about, Winston Churchill or any of the other celebrities. We had our own heroes.

To begin with air raids were regular events, starting in October 1939. The drill varied depending on where you were at the time. The theory was that as soon as the siren started wailing you were supposed to go to some designated place of safety, but in truth that was not the normal practice. At home we usually put out the lights, opened the blinds and watched whatever there was to see. If it was really exciting, as it often was, we went outside for a better view. There was a particular raid that comes to mind that occurred when we were sledging out at Waterfield brae. As soon as the siren went we headed for Eastbank where family friends, the Firths, stayed, and from there we had a grandstand view of the action over Scapa. What we saw was not bombs falling or exploding, but hundreds of shells from the fleet and the many heavy anti-aircraft batteries surrounding the base bursting in the sky like some massive firework display, along with thousands of tracer bullets, which left trails of light behind them as they streamed up into the darkness. The whole drama was illuminated by the many huge searchlights playing their rays around like some glorious display of the 'Merry Dancers' (aurora borealis). Spectacular it was, of course, and the accompanying din added dramatically to the whole effect. It was well-named the Scapa 'barrage'.

Moyra, as a small girl, had an even better view from her grandparents' home at Lynnfield in Holm, where they overlooked the Flow from fairly close range, and like us they viewed the whole proceedings from outside. Her outstanding memory of air raids, however, was the drill in the house in Victoria Street, where she lived. She and her mother - her dad was in the army - were told just to come down to the ground floor area as soon as the siren went where it would be safer. The other tenants were told the same, but to add to the confusion the family in the top flat had an old dog and a much-valued collection of prize canaries. Every time the warning came Bobby began his trek up and down the three flights, firstly with the dog and family and then one

by one with the birdcages. By the time he
got the last one down the all clear was
usually sounding and the whole 'shebang'
had to be carted up again. The dog, old and
crabbit, was first down and last up, much to
the discomfort of the others as it had a
tendency to bite if you went near it.

Air raid precautions

At school we were alerted for air raids or
practice drills by an alarm bell fitted in every
classroom. When it went off we shot to our feet and made an 'orderly' exit. As we had regular
practice drills we were well aware of how unpleasant it was being packed like sardines in dark
smelly shelters. Therefore, when the real thing came, those of us who lived nearby headed for
home. We usually stayed home if it was getting close to school closing time when the 'all clear'
went. This practice for some reason never engendered more than a 'rollicking' from the teachers
or the headmaster.

One bonus that came our way was additional holidays until air raid shelter provision was
made. (An exciting rumour spread round the school that there was a German spy hiding in the
girls' shelters. If they smelt anything like ours he was welcome to them.) As the war progressed
and the futility of sending bombers over such a well-guarded base as Scapa became apparent to
the German Luftwaffe, the raids tapered off, with only spasmodic and fairly ineffective sorties. To
us, they were a miss. Mind you, it was scary at times and the excitement did not mean that we
were not happy to hear the 'all-clear' blaring.

We all carried gas masks of course, in little cardboard boxes fitted into shoulder bags which
were supposed to go everywhere with us. Regular gas mask drills at school made sure that we
knew how to put them on in a hurry if required. There was a peculiar rubbery smell with them,
which still brings gas masks to mind if I catch a whiff of anything made of rubber today. Green
painted boards were set up everywhere, which we were told would turn orange if there was any
gas about. Sensibly, they did not put any near the boys' shelters.

Thankfully, evacuation from areas considered to be likely targets of German bombers was
never an issue in Orkney, in spite of Scapa Flow. Some evacuees did come to Orkney, however,
mainly from big cities on the mainland to relatives or friends, and in the main they settled in
very quickly.

We were encouraged to buy National Savings Certificates, which we stuck in special books,
the money going to help with the war effort.

From time to time news came back, mostly via the school, that someone from Orkney had
been killed or wounded, and even if we did not know them personally we often knew a younger
brother or a sister. It brought the real dangers of war closer to us.

The gloom over Orkney at the news that the *Royal Oak* had been torpedoed and sunk when
at anchor in Scapa Flow was felt by all ages. At six years old you do not understand the full
horror of such an event. No doubt we were protected from that to a degree but I remember
going with my Dad in Bertie Rendall's car, out to the cliffs at Gaitnip and seeing part of the
warship's side still protruding above water before she finally settled on to the seabed. Naturally
everybody was speaking about it, especially as the full scale of the tragedy became clearer, but
the real meaning of it did not sink in until we were much older. Rumours abounded of course
and suggestions of local help to guide the submarine in, IRA sabotage, etc, were passed around,
but the simple truth was that a daring U-boat captain, Gunther Prien had managed to get into
the Flow, fire his torpedoes and out again, unscathed. It triggered off a new hive of activity and
piles of construction workers, supported later by about a thousand Italian prisoners-of-war
captured in North Africa, suddenly appeared on the streets. They were there to build the
Churchill Barriers from Holm to South Ronaldsay, completely sealing off the eastern approaches
to the Flow.

The Italians added a new dimension to local life; people from another country, speaking a
'funny' language that we did not understand (and what they made of the Orcadian dialect is

anybody's guess). We thought we were very clever and sophisticated when we shouted, 'Italiano mucho malo,' (which we believed meant 'Italians very bad') after them, ready if necessary to run for dear life, but they only smiled. Later, when Italy surrendered and they were no longer 'prisoners' they also integrated into the community and were allowed a remarkable amount of freedom to move around at will, even visiting local houses. They had a cracking football team. Soon they became as familiar on the street in their dark uniforms as the British servicemen had become. Occasionally, and understandably, incidents would occur when our own lads came home on leave from Italy, perhaps even released from an Italian prisoner-of-war camp. Seeing how well-off the Italians seemed to be, they would get a bit annoyed, with the inevitable result. We only watched and wondered. The legacy they left, the barriers and the chapel they built for themselves, is still very much part of our heritage now; the barriers are a highway into town for those in the South Isles, and the chapel is a poignant reminder of their stay here, and what people are really like when war does not divide us.

Other preparations that we were familiar with were the activities of the Civil Defence under the stewardship of 'Pop' Doloughan. There were displays in the school playground of the use of stirrup pumps and other equipment, with hands-on participation encouraged for all ages. Another drill, organised under this umbrella along with the Red Cross, was the rescuing of 'casualties' from a bombed building, when some of us 'volunteered' to be tied to a stretcher and lowered out of an upstairs window above Liptons (now 'We Frame It') to the ground below. We were then whisked away for 'treatment' in a building at the bottom of The Strynd where we were fêted with tea and a biscuit. Nothing like that happens any more.

The Home Guard added their contribution to the proceedings and by all accounts 'Dad's Army' was just as relevant in Orkney as anywhere else. A large percentage of Orcadians were exempt from call-up if they were deemed necessary for agricultural or other essential work. Many of them were excellent shots, something that goes along with living in rural areas where a substantial part of the daily diet came from what was brought home. They were also, due to their lifestyle, hardy and competent in many practical skills. Discipline, however, drill and similar military necessities were not their strong point. Manoeuvres intended to be serious training for coping with wartime situations, frequently became a game, sometimes even a farce. The challenge, 'Bang! Bang! You're dead,' was known to engender the reply, 'Choog! Choog! I'm a tank.' A whole book could be written about the exploits of the Home Guard in Orkney.

On the non-military side there was a lot going on. Fortunes were made and lost; the black market was doing well with deals between service personnel and some local traders very active. We also had ration books, of course, obtainable from the Food Office at the foot of East Road, and each family had to register with one grocer. Extras were sometimes available for regular customers, from 'under the counter', and the odd sweetie was often slipped our way from a friendly shop owner. Most town dwellers had enough relatives and friends in the country and island districts to boost their supplies considerably. Lack of fresh fruit was a problem and when it reappeared after the war it was such a treat. Big Jaffa oranges, grapefruit, bananas, melons, etc, were things that most of us could barely remember. The sight of a banana was almost too much to contemplate and some were not sure what to do with it, though lots of suggestions were offered. Corn flakes, formerly called 'post toasties', were fabulous. Wheat flakes never had the same attraction. The day that sweets came off the ration there was almost a riot in the sweet shops. Every available penny was assembled to spend on this luxury and Mrs Allan had to impose her own form of 'rationing' until she could get in enough supplies to cope. The wartime ration for a month came nowhere near satisfying the average child's sweet tooth, so we supplemented this with home-made toffee (not often, as the ingredients such as Nestlé's milk and sugar were also subject to rationing); raisins, currants, crystallised sugar lumps (used for baking), 'Zubes', Victory Vs and various other cough sweets, *peedie* black things called 'Imps', Horlicks tablets, etc. All in all we were not deprived; we just moaned.

The other form of 'rationing' affected clothes; each person had an annual coupon allowance for clothing and footwear. This never seemed to be a problem, as clothes lasted a while and got darned or patched when necessary. Clothes were handed down and fashion was hardly an issue.

The only things I felt deprived of were rubber boots and plimsolls - the latter not high on my mother's list of priorities for me, but very high on mine. Boy, what I would have given - had I had it to give - for a pair of black, or better still white, gym shoes. The day that Geordo Borwick turned up at school sporting a brand new pair of white *plimmies* he was the envy of every boy in the playground. Because of the nature of their work, people who lived on farms got special permits for rubber boots, and often relatives or friends outwith the farming community benefited from this. One peculiar ruling was that those with big feet got extra coupons. Everybody's feet at that age grew but for some reason those with more than the normal grip on mother earth were given this particular perk.

Orkney was never better off for entertainment. Intended to boost troop morale, we had the benefit of all the top stars; Vera Lynn, definitely the greatest singer of all time, Gracie Fields, Tommy Handley, Yehudi Menuhin, George Formby and many others. We got the lot. Clearly we did not see all these great stars, but via friendly servicemen and women we did see some. ENSA concerts were top class even if some of the performers were not household names. The huge garrison theatre at Hatston, where Ortak is now, the theatre up at the RAF camp off Holm Road, where the cheese factory was and the Naval Cinema, now the Arts Theatre, were familiar places to us. Every taste was catered for from slapstick to opera, something that contained an element of risk. One famous story concerned the tenor in a piece of opera who was manfully singing the question, 'Where shall I put it? Where shall I put it?' when, mercifully, a sergeant, showing remarkable presence of mind, shot to his feet and in a voice that could be heard throughout the entire theatre threatened, 'The first *!*!* that opens his mouth goes on a charge.' Not all service personnel or civilians were opera buffs.

Camp concerts, produced by the troops themselves, were great entertainment. There were many talented people among them and to know someone on the stage added a bit of spice to the show. At the RAF station up at the old creamery they went to great lengths to produce an annual pantomime for the local kids. They knew exactly how to get us involved and managed to provide refreshments as well. We had a great time.

To get into the Naval Cinema you had to be escorted by someone from the services, but this was not much of a problem. All you had to do was hang around the door long enough, looking miserable, and some soft-hearted 'Wren' would take you in. I remember sitting bored out of my mind through about three-and-a-half hours of *Citizen Kane* with Orson Welles in the starring role. Served me right.

Parties on camp were not uncommon, particularly at Christmas, when local children, especially those connected with any of the service personnel on camp, were royally entertained with games and food. It may have relieved the boredom for servicemen at times and it did wonders for us. Some of this talent must have spilled over to the locals and the Kirkwall Arts Club was formed in 1944 with the support of Donald Hewlitt of *It ain't half hot Mum* fame. They had premises in the 'Toc H' on Great Western Road.

Parties in the home frequently included friends from the forces, and the odd rum ration or a glass of *home brew* helped to liven things up. We played such exotic games as 'Murderers' or 'Sardines'; we danced, had singsongs, etc, and we even used to get a small glass of *home brew* on occasions, as it was never looked upon as being 'drink'.

Some of the craft exhibitions laid on by servicemen during the war were amazing. Orcadians, many of whom had 'good hands', thoroughly enjoyed seeing new skills in arts and crafts produced by some very talented people. One particular item that comes to mind was a large model, bigger than the usual doll's house, of St Magnus Cathedral, made entirely out of matchsticks. It must have taken ages, and even collecting enough matchsticks must have been some task. Local crafts began to take on new ideas: cigarette lighters made out of bullet shells, model battleships, air-sea rescue launches, Spitfires, etc. My Uncle Jim made dozens of destroyers and sold them to servicemen in Shapinsay to take home.

We made parachutes out of hankies or bits of cloth with a length of string at each corner, adding some weight to make them work properly. They were then dropped from any high point available, or rolled up and thrown up in the air as high as possible, in the hope that they would unravel on the way down. Another thing that we made was a small 'submarine', which consisted of a shaped piece of wood with a bit of lead attached. The weight of the lead had to be worked out by trial and error so that when dropped in water it would submerge for a time and then slowly work its way back to the surface. Toy rifles, made out of wood, took the place of bows and arrows and if we had acquired an army cap of some sort, so much the better.

Sport, particularly football, was at an all time high during and just after the war. Always keen participants in sport, Orcadians benefited enormously from the influx of talented footballers, some of them professional. The late Sir Matt Busby was a PTI at Stanger Head camp for a time and quite a number of professionals played regularly in the local league and cup competitions for Hatston, the aerodrome just on the outskirts of Kirkwall. Names like Lucas, Ogden, Dickie Yates, spring to mind. They were the main influence but one proud boast we have is that no matter how many players they drafted in, and they did whenever they needed to, they never succeeded in winning the Orkney League. Orcadian footballers were learning fast. The Italians also had some very talented players and later there were quite a number of Poles working in Orkney who also produced their share of footballers. The Scottish Command with Tommy Walker of Hearts and Scotland included, took in Orkney as part of their tour, and played against the Orkney Defences at Hatston.

Songs from the war were very popular. We all sang rude songs about Hitler with great enthusiasm. Song sheets with all the words were available from Leonards, so we knew them all. The *Blighty* was a fairly racy magazine for the time, and though it would have been produced with servicemen in mind it was a regular addition to most houses. *The Illustrated London News* and *The Picture Post* were also widely read, or more accurately, scanned, as they consisted mainly of pictures from the various fields of warfare, and, of course, every Friday evening we queued up for the weekly edition of *The Daily Mirror* which arrived on the ferry, *St Ola*. Maps showing the latest situation on the various war fronts were also common wall decorations in Orkney households.

It all had to end sometime. VE day was a great day with everyone laughing and chatting, even cheering sometimes. Kirkwall was full of little boys, maybe some girls too, shinning up

War and peace - Scapa

downpipes, clinging on to *spoots*, tying up ropes or string from which flags and bunting were suspended. Everybody took part in the celebrations. Some months later, after VJ day, my sister was in the geography class at KGS when several of Orkney's 'Burma Boys' came in; Jim Dowell, Gus Harcus and Tiny Leonard among them. They were going round the various classes giving all the female teachers a big hug. She said it was a picture to see the geography teacher, Miss Bella Bichan, not the most cuddlesome person in the world, laughing, with tears rolling down her cheeks, happy to see them all safely home. The good times were back.

Several years had yet to pass before things got back to the old 'normal', and in fact things never were quite the same again - too much had happened. The thousands of visiting servicemen and women began to leave, except those who decided to settle here. Gradually our own lads and lasses came home. Most of the camps were dismantled and the huts auctioned, apart from those that were retained for conversion later into temporary houses. Buildings taken over by the military were restored to their original owners, some vastly improved. People could move around freely again without permits. Food and clothing came off rationing. This new situation was in some ways harder for us to get used to. Things were so quiet.

School . . .

Schools are decidedly different now. New subjects, new technology, mean that some of the old methods are invalid and have been abandoned or changed. Classrooms are much more 'informal' - bedlam might be too strong a word - but it is hard to imagine what Miss Harvey, or Miss Bichan, would have made of the present set up.

Once you were in your 'lines' ready to go into the classroom, you were expected to keep your mouth shut unless asked a question. Even whispering was frowned upon. It was easier to enforce then with the backup of the dreaded strap, used with impunity by some teachers, but not always fairly. Getting the strap when your hands were frozen, as they often were in winter, was very painful even if it did warm them up. One lad, Bruce Flett, will never have forgotten his first day at school. He was seated right in front of the table with his eyes fixed on a big red apple, which was to be the teacher's 'play-piece'. She had to go out for something and the temptation proved too much for Bruce. He took a large bite out of it, just one, but it was enough. Two of 'the best' was his punishment and a timely warning to us all that things were different at school. The cane, used in some schools at that time, was not used in Kirkwall while I was there.

Learning the alphabet from a little book with gems like, 'P is for Peter with a pack on his back', containing a picture of Peter and his pack, was quite straightforward. Sums were not too bad as we chanted the tables together; 'Two times one is two, Two times two is four', and so on. Copying copperplate writing was a nightmare for some. We had special notebooks for this exercise, but with paper in short supply we mostly wrote on slates with slate pencils, which could make the most irritating, *scruttling* noise if you worked at it. One side of the slate was lined for writing and the other plain for drawing or sums. Writing with a slate pencil was not all that easy. They did not slide smoothly over the surface and soon became blunt, and they frequently broke if you leaned a little too heavily. Writing with a blunt stump tended to leave a bit of a mess. Sharpening the pencil with a knife was the only hope, but it was not very successful.

Kirkwall Grammar School

The Strynd showing K.G.S.

Music in the infant school meant singing and banging 'musical' things such as triangles, tambourines, cymbals and other percussion instruments. Teachers must have dreaded music lessons. Art was drawing pictures in a tray of sand, weaving paper mats, or, on rare occasions, colouring with small, hard, square-shaped crayons kept in long shaped tins. PE consisted of games outside, or inside if the weather was bad. Little changed as we moved up the primary, though we did progress to pencils and jotters, which we had to supply. For tests we had exercise books with red covers, which remained in the classroom and had to be kept tidy. Using a pen with a split nib was a nightmare. It worked fine on the down stroke but on the upstroke it usually dug in and stuck, making a blot on the paper which meant you were in deep trouble. There was no Tippex to save the day, and rubbing out with an 'ink' rubber usually resulted in a hole in the page.

Blind demo

One 'lesson', given by Miss Bichan in primary 8, left its mark on her more than on us. She was giving a demonstration of how a blind person found his or her way around. She was to pass through the open classroom door, and to her eternal credit, if not her well being, she confidently approached the opening with arms outstretched and eyes tight shut. Unfortunately her left arm went to one side of the door and her right arm to the other and her face led her quite firmly into the edge. The word 'blind' took on a new meaning that day.

It was also in her class that the rudiments of correct English became much clearer when she questioned the grammatical correctness of a sentence in one pupil's essay. The explanation from one of the class was, 'Please Miss, she's geen and patten putten where she should hiv pitten put.'

FIRST INFANTS 1938 – K.G.S.

Back row: Miss Harvey; Moira Bews; Thora Walker; Mary Ann Bremner; Betty Mackenzie; Alison Lennie; Isobel Couper; Ena Hadden

Middle row: Alan Croy; Lily Newlands; Bruce Flett; Ashley Rosie; Ida Nicolson; Jack Donaldson; Helen Leslie; Jim Robertson; Inga Flett; Alistair Smith; Madge Wilson; Gillian May; Andrew Muir; Ian Cheyne.

Front row: Ian Gray; Megan Kelday; Lennie Douglas; Marjorie Omand; Hughie Donaldson; Margaret Borwick; Willa Fox; John Gray; Self; _____ _____

After leaving the infant department, progress through the primary school was either through classes 1, 3, 5, 7, or 2, 4, 6, 8. Teachers varied enormously: some were 'tartars', some gentle; but the school 'intelligence' system kept us well-informed of what to expect when moving up. Some of them had taught our parents as well. It was frequently a job for life, mainly for women, and most of them were spinsters.

Good class attendance merited ' the banner'; a triangular piece of cloth that entitled us to get out half an hour early on Friday and which was then hung proudly in the classroom for the following week. This caused some problems when parents of big families depended on the smaller children being escorted home by the older ones. It would cause real problems now with so many working mothers, childminders and so on. Primary 6 proved to be a bit different in as much as we had no regular teacher but were subjected to a whole range of 'temps', including female and male teachers seconded from the 'big' school. We had our first taste of Mr Gow, one of the maths teachers from the 'Higher Grade', and it was a bit of a shock, especially for one lad who was not paying attention. Mr Gow went slowly up the far side of the room talking all the time, along the back and down the passageway to where this lad was giggling and fooling around. Without warning, he landed such a rattle behind the boy's ear we wondered if his head would stay on. It did, and it snivelled for the rest of the afternoon while we all gave our undivided attention to every word that was said. That couldn't happen now, and with the banning of the strap all forms of corporal punishment have gone. Assaults with chalk, rulers, pointers, books, blackboard dusters etc, are no longer permitted. Whether this has improved schools or not I will leave readers to decide.

Free school milk was introduced, establishing a new 'elite' - the milk monitors. Their task for the week was to hand round trays containing the tin cups of milk, collect them when empty, and wash them in cold water out in the washroom. This scheme was very popular and most of us took advantage of it.

CLASS PHOTO K.G.S. - c. 1943/44
Back row: Irene Peace; Maureen Newlands; Helen Leslie; Ena Hadden; Margaret Ormiston; Ellen Anderson; Elaine Muir; Isobel Couper; Evelyn Rosie; Lena Kirkpatrick; Mona Tait
Second row from back: Vivian Hourston; Colin MacGillivray; Ivan Kelday; Jackie Walker; Ron Wilson; Colin Moar; John Flett; Rennie Eunson; Olaf Herdman; John Bews; Jim Robertson; Jim Firth
Second row from front: Ella Rendall; Jean Corsie; Betty Mackenzie; Meta Marwick; Lila Wards; Alison Lennie; Moira Sabiston; Margaret Scollay; Ann Mooney; Moira McLeod; Vera Muir; Thora Walker
Front row: Self; Jack Sinclair; George Borwick; Ian Gray; Ian Swanney

Pee-heeing with the teacher in the infant and primary schools was common. Girls brought in posies of primroses or other wild flowers while boys usually took in *brandies* to be set among all the other jars of dead or dying fish and flowers in the classroom window.

Pee-heeing

Except for the smaller chairs and desks in the infant department, classrooms were similar all through school. Warmth was always a problem. In each room there was a large coal fire in one corner next to the door, almost entirely blocked off by the teacher's desk and chair. What little heat filtered through benefited only those who by their efforts were at the bottom of the class, while those who worked hard and reached the 'top' were planted at the back, suffering from nail cold, frozen feet, chattering teeth and runny noses. It did not offer much incentive.

Classrooms were austere places with high ceilings. The walls, apart from those that were wood and glass sliding partitions, were covered in dark varnished lining to about a third of the way up, and the rest was a dull coloured distemper. Two or three enormous windows let in light and cold. Floors were bare wood. Other features were wooden vents, which had to be opened with the window pole, a large, long case clock and an alarm bell. Furnishings, from primary school up, included double desks made of oak and cast iron with a folding top and seat, and underneath a bit intended for books, which was always used for rubbish. Inkwells were fitted into a hole in the top, and a groove was provided for a pen or pencil. For the teacher there was a desk and chair, a large blackboard, which slid up and down, and a lockable cupboard for supplies.

The discomfort was increased for some by the distance they had to travel to get to school. There were no school buses, few cars or bikes, and not too many ponies and traps available. 'Shanks's mare' was the order of the day and it was a fair old trek if you lived at Work, Carness, Berstane, above the golf course, or other remote places around Kirkwall. Tramping several miles in driving wind, rain, sleet or snow, frequently in the dark, was commonplace, and meant sitting all day soaking wet, or at best damp, before making the same trip home after school in the dark. They had to take extra food as well as there were no luxuries like school dinners. Late-coming was of course a 'crime' and the strap was used freely as a spur to punctuality, regardless of the distance or the weather. No wonder some of them were tempted to *skin* school at times.

The primary playground was a small rectangle surrounded by classrooms, with a huge porch in the middle of one side, and a cast iron fire escape in the corner. Not much sun got in but it was sheltered, and the fire escape was an added attraction to the more acrobatic. Schoolbags never seemed to last long - they were not designed to double up as footballs or projectiles. This was especially true in the big school, when at break times they were launched from the stair landing to join the pile in the corner below.

As for the toilets, or in school parlance the *cogs*, primitive is a word that would flatter them. A shallow channel on the floor that ran full length along one wall, and a row of open cubicles with wooden seats suspended over running water along the opposite wall, was the total provision for the whole male student population of the school. The provision for girls ran along similar lines. On occasions, if someone was ill, he or she was allowed to use the teachers' proper flush toilets. The air raid shelters were dark and therefore slightly more private - unless the air raid siren went. There was no hot water, no soap, towels, toilet rolls, not even a *Press and Journal*. Again, this was not too bad if you could go home at lunchtime, but many could not. Drinking water was available in cast iron cups chained to cast iron pumps, installed at strategic places around the playgrounds.

Promotion to the 'big' school, or 'Higher Grade' was a big day. The syllabus changed and we went to different classrooms and teachers every three-quarters of an hour. Gym in the hall, new interesting places like the woodwork room, the science labs, the domestic science room, a proper art room, etc, all helped to give a whole new outlook to school, at least for a while. The day started with a blast on a whistle, which summoned us to form lines. This was usually under the control of Mr Gow, and you did not delay. Climbing the stairs for the first time after morning assembly was a bit daunting. We felt big enough, most of the lads having been promoted to long *breeks*, (some that fitted but most that didn't). We had heard something of what to expect from older brothers and sisters or friends but with so much that was new it took a bit of getting used to. Even finding the right classroom could cause a problem, especially if you were late, and trying to assess each new teacher was almost as difficult as coming to terms with entirely new subjects. Things like French, Latin, algebra, geometry, science, woodwork, commercial subjects, domestic science, were all new fields for us. Even geography and history, which we had touched on in primary school, suddenly became full-blown subjects in their own right with specialist teachers. Only arithmetic and English seemed to offer some sort of natural progression.

Mr Leask, the headmaster, was a real eye-opener. Affectionately known to the entire school as 'Sando'- but not to his face, I must add - he had that wonderful mix of voice and stature that made the toughest pupil shrivel, accompanied by a heart of gold. He knew every pupil, their background and potential, and all were considered to be of equal worth in his eyes. His presence was felt throughout the whole school. He would burst into a classroom, unannounced, wipe everything, no matter how important, off the blackboard and scribble something on it that required an answer. Then he stood glowering at the class, thumbs hooked in his waistcoat, before thrusting a finger in the direction of some unfortunate. Not a word had been spoken, and as soon as he got the answer he desired he vanished with a flourish, leaving the poor teacher to try to continue the interrupted lesson. Nobody was really scared of 'Sando', unless they had done something beyond the pale, but we did hold him in awe.

After morning assembly, latecomers to the 'big school' were let in by 'Sando', each one getting a 'verbal' on the way past. Occasionally he would grab someone by the ear with the booming demand, 'Give me five reasons why you're late, Robertson.' (The particular Robertson in question, who lived some distance out of town and had a milk round to do with his dad each morning before school, will, I am sure, recognise himself.) Occasionally when the regular teacher was off, Mr Leask took science, which was his subject. In spite of the obvious risks involved, when he turned round to write something on the blackboard beakers sailed across the lab, but it was the receiver who usually copped it, if he or she missed the catch, not the thrower. He rarely *strapped*, and if he did it was painful but most assuredly deserved.

Five reasons Robertson

Another occasion when Mr Leask came into the picture was when our 'football' was kicked over the boys' shelters into his garden. Whoever put it there had to retrieve it. After a tentative knock on the door you were led through the sitting room and out through the back door, being *bawled out* every step of the way, only to get a smile and a biscuit on the way back from the kindly Mrs Leask. She was a wonderful person, involved in every kind of helpful or charitable cause imaginable. She was also a Sunday School teacher. They really were an amazing couple.

In primary and infant schools all our teachers were known by their proper names; Miss Harvey, Miss Leask, Miss Shearer, or whatever; but in the 'Higher Grade' we discovered that many of them had nicknames, and were referred to by this name at all times provided they were not within earshot. There were 'Foostie', 'Malint', 'Onions', 'Merro Bun', 'Twitter' and so on. I don't doubt they all knew and accepted it as part of school life. As long as they continued to teach, and even after they had left school, the names were passed down the generations. They also fell into various categories: those who ruled with a rod of iron; those who had favourites; gifted ones; useless ones; etc. They were treated with respect outside the school as well as in class. All in all, they gave us as good a chance as any, and I believe we ended up as capable as those finishing school now.

Another amazing discovery in the 'big' school was that people carved their names on desks. Carved is maybe a bit strong though some attempts with a penknife were in evidence, but digging your name into a soft area of wood that had not already been used, with a blunt pencil, was a regular practice. Careful study revealed names of people nearer our parents' ages, who had passed through these hallowed chambers. Even my older sister, whom I had always looked upon as a paragon of virtue, had defaced several desks. You did not put a date after it of course, as it may have been traced as 'new' - that is assuming that teachers spent much of their spare time examining each desk in their particular classroom in minute detail, recording any new additions, and planning suitable retribution. It was not quite graffiti but about as near as we got. It was more of an addition to the KGS's rich tapestry.

The strap, also known as the *clipe,* or more correctly the tawse, was something that was familiar to kids for many years, but for the uninitiated it may be worthy of some explanation. It consisted of a piece of leather approximately twenty-four inches long, with one half split into three or four 'tails', which whistled when it was wielded by an expert. Width and thickness varied, but the worst ones - from a pupil's point of view - were at least one quarter of an inch thick and not more than one and a quarter inches wide, while the best ones were about one eighth of an inch thick and about two inches wide. The results varied enormously. Some teachers administered it with relish, with their full weight and strength, and were not too fussy about where they hit, hand or wrist. Others had little will or ability to use it, and if they had been supplied with one of the lighter variety, then the punishment was not much of a worry. The number of strokes also varied according to the offence and the mood of the teacher. Different techniques were used, from holding out one hand to holding out both, one on top of the other, or, worst of all, laying your hand on the desk. The second and third methods were designed to stop you from *clicking* your hand out of the way, a natural and instinctive reaction which often led to the teacher leathering his or her own legs. When this happened it did not improve the teacher/pupil relationship, and there was only one loser with further strokes of the *clipe* inevitable.

The strap

King Street - the way to school

In most cases the punishment, though painful, was acceptable, even amusing at times, but there were teachers who went way over the top, and badly swollen hands and wrists were not uncommon in certain classes. One particular teacher who had succeeded in breaking a boy's wrist with the belt was banned from having one in his classroom, but this did not stop him from borrowing from another teacher when he felt so inclined. One lad, who had been sent for a strap, came back with one of the lighter variety, and for his pains he got it across the face before being sent for a 'proper' one. Occasionally, if no one admitted to a particular offence, the whole class got belted. *Tell-pies* or *clipes* were not very popular, but the offender usually got his or her 'come-uppance' later in the playground for not owning up. Mr Fettes, our music teacher, was a zealous *cliper*, and this tendency was not improved when he once discovered his strap hanging on top of the wall clock, well out of his reach.

Having said all this, there were teachers who hardly ever used this form of deterrent; they did not have to. Their presence was enough to generate total attention. One science teacher, Mr Goodall, was one of those who had to be watched. As soon as he entered the room, if he was looking serious there was no problem, but if he came in with a smile on his face you could look out. Someone was going to catch it. Mr Harcus, the woodwork teacher, had pieces of wood to add to his armoury, which he either threw at you or whacked you with.

I mentioned getting the belt from Mr Leask, the headmaster. It only happened to me once following another form of retribution not all that uncommon at that time. It happened in the English class on someone's birthday, and during the good wishes that were being passed on I 'toasted' the girl's good health with an inkwell. Unfortunately as I returned the inkwell to its hole in the desk some ink got spilt on the floor. Sitting in the front row immediately behind the spill, when the teacher came in and enquired as to who had done it, there was no way I could avoid accepting the blame. Her reaction, however, surprised me as it did the rest of the class, and it

CLASS PHOTO K.G.S. – c. 1946/47
Back row: Jim Gibson; Roy Bichan; Dave Linklater; Robert Chalmers; Tommy Tulloch; Sandy Firth; John Bews; Bill Stevenson; Rognvald Scott; Alistair Smith
Second row from back: Thora Walker; Ena Hadden; Margaret Flett; Annie Drever; Ann Mooney; Freda Brown; Dorothy Robertson; Elsie Berstan; Catherine Johnson; Zena Young; Marion Baikie; Nona Mackay
Second row from front: Mariannie Bias; Jenny Scott; Marion Moodie; Anna May Rosie; Mona Tait; Cathy Crisp; Margaret Horne; Mollie Shearer; Maisie Robertson; Margaret Leonard; Isobel Couper
Front row: Jimmy Firth; Eric Moodie; Wilson Laird; Ian Gray; Self; John Thomson

certainly surprised Ron Sabiston as well, who was going round with the class attendance registers at the time. The door was thrown open, my schoolbag hurled into the corridor, cleaning the legs from under the unfortunate Ron, and I was ordered to follow and not to come back. I did try the following morning but it was no go and I spent the following two weeks down in the pegs area trying to work out what to do. The decision was finally taken out of my hands as I was spotted, reported and summoned to the headmaster's office. He made enquiries and whatever story he was told convinced him that I deserved six of the belt, and I was ordered back to the class with the instruction that if I caused any more problems I should be sent to him and not expelled from the class. This could not happen now and an opportunity would be given to explain your side of the story before any action was taken. I think the incident reflected more on the teacher than it did on me.

Discipline problem

Homework was almost a kind of punishment and rarely received the attention it merited. There were so many things to do after school, and as some of us had part-time jobs as message boys it either got rushed, or, if you were stuck, copied. This practice was frequently spotted by the appropriate teacher and earned the belt. 'Lines' were another form of punishment, and anything to ease the burden was tried. Getting a pal to write some in 'your handwriting' or by using black carbon paper often got past a casual inspection by a teacher more interested in the inconvenience caused than the actual result.

There were subjects that were universally popular. To the studious, I suppose, they all came into that category, but PE to the agile was always fun. A game we played a lot was unique, as far as I know, to KGS, played in the playground with 'goals' at either end. It was called 'Hurly-Burly' and was a sort of combination of basketball and rugby, where you could run with the ball until touched, when you had to pass it. There was no kicking, and scoring was achieved by throwing the ball past the goalkeeper. The number of players was dictated simply by the size of the class.

Gym in the hall using mats and an assortment of apparatus, such as a horse, box, beam and

Hurly burly in the snow c. 1945/46
Back row: John Bews; Roy Thomson; John Paterson
Front row: John Thomson; Russell Groundwater; Ian Gray; Self; Alistair Smith

spring board, was a real treat. That was, apart from the entire term that the lads from secondary 4, 5 and 6 were made to march round the hall for the full three-quarters of an hour each gym period, doing the 'grand-march' variations. This was a punishment imposed by Mr Harcus, the woodwork teacher (who was doubling as gym teacher) because some of the boys refused to play for the house football teams if they were playing for one of the local clubs that same evening. His argument was, 'I don't want to give you too many strenuous exercises in case it spoils your performance.' He had his good side though, acquiring Charlie Chaplin films, which we were allowed to watch in the woodwork room after school. He also did an excellent impersonation of Charlie Chaplin on stage at many of the local shows, and also at the annual hockey match between senior girls and staff. He was something of a character. He had been a footballer of some ability at both club and county level, but I always remember his explanation of how to kick a ball low into the wind, which he chose to demonstrate by kicking it with the wind, just in case. I also remember him insisting on some of us older boys trying out his new Vespa motorcycle in the playground. Some of the lads had some experience and were mechanically minded. I was not, and a good relationship almost vanished when I nearly ran into the woodwork room wall. Fortunately the bike and I both ended up in a heap just short of collision. Braking and 'throttling' were both very much on his mind for a moment or two before peace was restored.

Gym shoes deserve a mention. Due to 'rationing' few pupils had their own *plimmies,* but the school must have had an allocation, which bore no resemblance to requirements. As soon as you walked in through the hall door you smelt them - hundreds of plimsolls piled in cupboards around the hall. There was always a mad stampede when we were told to get changed. The ideal was to find a matching pair of slip-ons of the right size, all in one piece. At a guess this may have been achieved about once a term. Most of the time you did your PE lined up in rows, wearing two left shoes of different sizes, one slip-on, one lacing and with half the soles hanging off. Add this to the assortment of clothes picked with 'growing room' in mind, or 'hand-me-downs' that never quite fitted; we must have looked like Mary Poppins's penguins.

Ready for PE

Music was a bit of a pain really. Apart from our efforts in the infant department on the triangle and the tambourine, we had no tuition on musical instruments, not even a recorder. All we did was sing and not very attractive songs at that. We learned something about scales and clefs by memorising quotations such as, 'All Cows Eat Grass', to represent ACEG, or 'Every God Boy Deserves Favour', to remind us of EGBDF. We were also taught something about rhythm or beat, with recitations such as 'Ta Tiffy Ta Tiffy Taffa Tiffy Ta, Taffa Tiffy Taffa Tiffy Tatty Ta'. It must have been useful, but hardly the thing to inspire a budding John Lennon. Music could be a bit of a 'hoot' at times. There was one particular teacher who had a slot knitted into his crew-necked jumper to accommodate his tie. He had a passion for English folk-songs, and the 4th, 5th, and 6th year boys, many of them over six feet and weighing 17 stones who went to music together, were coached in *Nymphs and Shepherds Come Away,* and *Come Lasses and Lads get leave of your Dads and away to the Maypole High,* and other such delights. This we had to sing as a choir at the annual school concert. It could not have done a lot for the audience, apart from those with a mean sense of humour, and it certainly did nothing for us.

This music teacher was definitely a bit different, which became evident to me on one particular day. He had discovered that Mac Smith could play the piano very well, if reluctantly, and we were asked to remind him that Mac would play something for us during the next music period. To us this was great, a pleasant change from the usual lessons, and when he came in next day several hands shot up, but unfortunately mine was selected. He was by this time sitting at the piano, and when I passed on the reminder he told me to come out to the floor, asking me if I was trying to tell him how to run his class. He then grabbed me with the obvious intention of laying me across his knee and spanking me. He was not designed for such a move, and it was something he was not capable of doing without my full cooperation, which was certainly not forthcoming. He fell off the stool and we grappled for some time on the floor with me on top, until he suddenly realised his mistake. By this time I was visualising all sorts of retribution from a higher authority. Suddenly, he started to laugh, ordered me to my seat and then continued with the class as if nothing had happened. It was an odd experience. Mac was not invited to play. Maybe he thought the class had had enough entertainment for one day.

The science labs seemed to lend themselves to extra-curricular activities. There were six to eight large benches spaced round the rooms, with four gas taps in the centre of each to which we connected Bunsen burners when doing experiments. Something that was passed down the generations was that if you attached a tube to a spare tap, turned it on and blew hard, Bunsen burners all round the room would go out. This could cause some consternation in the middle of an experiment and also allowed gas from the unlit burners to flow into the room. Amazing what was considered to be amusing at times.

One science teacher, a large male of the species, used to punch you on the shoulder if you were not paying attention. On one occasion, while we were all seated in a circle round him, he found reason to exercise his usual retribution. Unfortunately, he punched a little too hard and the lad, perched on a stool, began to topple sideways, colliding with the boy alongside who in turn did the same, with the ultimate result that about a dozen stools and their occupants all followed one another in domino fashion, ending up in a heap on the floor. It was quite spectacular.

Science notebooks were a bit special, with hard covers containing paper with lines on one side of the page and graph sheets on the other. With paper in short supply we did not get new ones. My one had been partly used by Ina Hay (later Mrs Harcus), and as her work was somewhat tidier than mine it was often used by the teacher as a comparison - not, unfortunately, in my favour.

After a series of short-term appointments, including one with an Irish brogue and an atomic research specialist who are mentioned later, the appointment of a new science master came as a

SCHOOL TEAM (K.G.S.) 1949
Back row: Angus Baikie; Norrie Firth; Jimmy Sinclair; Alfie Flett
Middle Row: Jim Gibson; Robert Chalmers; Russell Groundwater; Self; Jim Robertson
Front row: John Flett; Bill Budge; Roy Bichan

bit of a shock. We had become a bit undisciplined, I guess, and it had become normal practice when thirsty to go to the tap and help ourselves to a drink of water. Unfortunately, I was the first one to develop a thirst, and even more unfortunately, the new teacher, Mr McKerron, was not in tune with this practice. Nothing was said until I returned to my seat, then he looked at me with two of the steeliest eyes I have ever seen, asked me what I thought I was doing, ignored my explanation and ordered me to his desk. I have heard of shooting from the hip, but he was the only teacher I ever saw who could belt from the hip. I never saw it coming but, by the powers, I knew when it arrived. He only delivered twice but it sent the message to me and to the rest of the class that things were about to be different. Our science improved dramatically. He was a fair man, a first class teacher and later headmaster; someone I grew to hold in the highest esteem both in and out of school.

Art was popular with most; drawing, colouring with crayons, using water-colours or poster paints on a variety of subjects, from still-life to interpreting 'what you felt' while listening to a piece of classical music. As you can imagine, that went down a bomb. On a rare afternoon when you had PE and double art, you could take your schoolbag home at lunchtime. That was a real treat. Woodwork for the boys, cooking and sewing for the girls, was looked forward to by most of us. However, the popularity or otherwise of any subject depended to a large degree on the teacher. Some had the knack of making the most boring subjects fun and that is when we learned most.

There were some optional subjects, where you could take additional periods of something you preferred instead of something you did not like. Instead of French, John Thomson and I took extra art, and as a privilege we were allowed out of school to go and sketch different subjects, such as the harbour, inside the Town Hall with its stained glass windows, the Cathedral, inside and out, and others. As you would expect we abused this privilege, and after a quick sketch of the designated topic we headed for Costie's and played snooker, or on one occasion badminton in the Town Hall, with members of the King Street Kirk club. Of course we were spotted, reported, belted and all privileges were withdrawn. I also took additional technical subjects instead of Latin, and due to a misunderstanding I missed out on technical drawing for a whole term, something that became very evident at exam time. It was considered to be my fault for not reporting the omission, so Mr Harcus rewarded me with a whole term doing nothing but technical drawing, to 'help' me to catch up. He never did anything by half. Woodwork, a favourite subject through the years, began with a pot stand and finished off with a tea trolley, which I still have.

Exam days were always a worry even for the brighter ones, who had ambitions to be top of the class and ultimately Dux. Most of us did not have that problem but it was a day of reckoning from which there was no escape. There was that nagging feeling that you should have swotted just a bit more, or even just a bit, but it was too late. It was important to pass at least so that you did not have the indignity of having to repeat a year. Great efforts were made to 'cram' at the last minute. You sat down and waited for the papers to be handed out, filled in your name and class at the top, and then when the OK was announced, you were away, writing feverishly as if your life depended on it, until suddenly you ran out of ideas and a lot of hopeful 'waffling' filled the remainder of the foolscap. Sometimes, if you finished early, you were allowed to leave, and then down in the shelters, the 'post mortem' began, trying to find out how many agreed with what you had put down, which did not help much. Nobody looked happy on exam days, not even the teachers.

The time came when the results were handed out; not always on the same day for each subject but when the teacher had managed to complete the correcting. The public way with which your papers were handed back with verbal as well as written comments, some of them quite scathing, did not do a lot for your morale unless you happened to be one of the 'elite'.

School was not all doom and gloom, however, far from it, and the popular saying that they were the best years of your life takes on more meaning the older you get. There were always enough 'smart Alecs' and incidents about to keep the balance. Teachers' 'bloomers' were latched on to (metaphorically speaking), and if they were real corkers they became part of KGS folklore.

A classic was the geography teacher, Miss Bichan's, instruction: 'Watch the map while I run over the mountains'; to those who knew her a most unlikely scenario; or, 'Watch the blackboard while I run through it', conjured up a classroom of hopeful faces. Then there was the instruction given to the pupil who enquired about borrowing a rubber, and was told to 'use the girl's behind'. We had an Irish science master with a very strong brogue, who used to delight us with the expression 'torty-tree and a turd' ('thirty-three and a third' in English).

The aforementioned Mr Gow, the senior maths teacher, had a fund of about three stories which he trotted out to generations of pupils for them to 'enjoy', almost on a weekly basis. 'I wouldn't like to be up there in that thing', observed Paddy, looking up at an aeroplane. 'I wouldn't like to be up there without it', was the reply that we all waited for before bursting into peals of laughter. We had a French teacher who always entered the classroom with the same instruction; 'Put away your knitting and your Hornby trains'. He was liked by most of us and we thought it would be OK to pelt him with snowballs on the way to school, convinced that he had a good sense of humour. That illusion quickly disappeared as we queued up to get belted when we got into the classroom. Education comes in all shapes and forms.

Teachers' 'romances', or 'advances' may be more accurate, amused us no end. Whenever a new male, bachelor teacher arrived in the 'big' school, certain members of the female staff changed noticeably in demeanour and dress. There were some quite glamorous female teachers who came and went as well. One redhead, Miss Barclay, who took science for a short time, is worthy of a mention, though her stay was short. During an experiment to make hydrogen, by dissolving zinc granules in hydrochloric acid inside a Wolf bottle, when it is the practice to light the hydrogen as it comes out but only after all the air has disappeared, she instructed one of us to light a match and try it. Unfortunately, it was too soon and the highly volatile mixture of air and hydrogen exploded. Girls and boys were running all over the classroom and out into the corridor with numerous facial cuts and burns. It took Mr Leask, the head, quite some time to restore order. She left to go into nuclear research.

Another attractive feature for us in the 'Higher Grade' was the sudden influx of kids from the rural districts and islands to pursue a level of education not available in the smaller schools. Many new and lasting friendships were fostered, and of course, there was a whole new batch of potential *clicks* for us *Toonies*. Initially they all stayed in private 'digs' round the town, but later the girls were all gathered together in the new girls' hostel, a collection of ex-army huts off Old Scapa Road, where they were strictly chaperoned by a matron and several female staff. They were not given a lot of freedom but they were allowed to have a party once a year, and it was a great honour to be invited, even though the invite was not signed by any individual. It was a bit like getting a Valentine card.

Apart from the academic side of things there were the fun times. Playtime usually involved a race to the Rocky shop, or down the Strynd to Davie Nick's for a sugary or creamy *cookie*. Some ran up accounts at the Rocky shop which were settled by Mums once a week. At lunch break it was football or nothing, usually with a small tennis ball. Those who did not play hung around the shelters chatting or smoking, which was popular at the time if you could afford it. Those who had no fags could be heard asking for 'a puff' or 'a couple'. There were no health warnings in those days.

School fights were regular affairs, mostly 'handbag' stuff with the ones that did the most shouting and swearing producing the least. There was lots of - 'Hold me back or I'll thump him, but for God's sake hold me back'. The shout of 'A fight, a fight!' was the signal for everybody to gather round the 'contestants' and start shouting for one or the other or both.

Sports days were a welcome break. Many of us entered races we had no hope of winning as we got extra time off to take part in the heats, which were run prior to sports day. Races were varied and catered for all age groups, culminating in the championship events to decide the boy and girl sports champions for the year. Lighter-hearted events included the pillow fight in which two contestants sat stride-legged over a heavy pole raised off the ground, and knocked lumps out of one another in an endeavour to unseat your opponent. Size did not always succeed in this event, which made it all the more attractive. The hockey matches that followed between girls and boys, or girls and staff, who usually turned up in fancy dress, were well supported.

The school magazine, *The Kirkwallian*, was always eagerly anticipated. We all got a chance to contribute and were delighted when we had something selected for inclusion by the magazine committee. One regular feature was 'apt quotations', which offered us the opportunity to have a wee go at one of the teachers. Having run for so long *The Kirkwallian* has become a very useful source of local social history.

On prize-giving day we all assembled in four classrooms with the partitions pulled back. The prize-winners from the different years were called out one by one to collect their prizes, be it for educational prowess or just good attendance, culminating in the awards to the school sports champions, and ultimately the school Dux.

The grand finale of the school year was the school dance, held each year at the end of the summer term. We bought tickets in advance or we did not get in, put on our best bib and tucker, boys in Sunday suits, girls in party frocks, and off we went. Obviously the big attraction was that it was one of the few chances that rival suitors had to dance with a particular girl, or girls generally, and hopefully escort one of them home. All the girls lined up on one side of the hall and the boys along the other, and when a dance was announced the boys made their way across the floor and invited their choice up to dance - unless it was a ladies' choice when the roles were reversed. Invited is maybe a bit strong as the usual approach rarely involved any verbal invitation, just a sort of beckoning with the head or hand, but always done with a hopeful smile. The main worry for the boys was that you might be rejected, and for girls, that you might not be asked up at all. Both were felt to be a great public humiliation. We hardly ever missed a dance. It was also a chance to be a bit of a 'wide boy' and dance with one of the female staff who had been brave enough to come along. It helped to release tensions between teachers and pupils, and some of the male teachers used to join the lads and chat informally. We had supper half-way through the evening, usually in the primary 8 classroom, and there was an ample supply of tea, sandwiches, sausage rolls, etc, to keep us going. There was no alcohol involved, not even surreptitiously as far as I remember, and drugs of course, were not yet around. It was just good innocent fun.

KGS holds happy memories for many people, and thanks to the education standards that were set, several of them went on to do great things

'The Shore' and roond aboot

Play - (or, what really mattered)

Touched on in other chapters, this, inevitably, has to be the biggest section. After all, for us kids it was what life was all about. School is fine, part-time jobs are handy for pocket money, but play, sports, games, generally enjoying yourself, that is what really matters at that age - and so it should be. There would be plenty of time to worry later.   Even the war had to take second place and fit around what we did. Games, outside and in, took up the lion's share of our time and the selection was endless, only limited by the imagination. Outdoors, in the backyard, in the playground, on the beaches or in the streets, activities were wide and varied and came in phases. On warm days we played in bare feet.

Timeless pastimes, like hide-and-seek, *peevers* , *picco* , rounders, skipping, with one or two ropes, French cricket, and many others, require no explanation. Some, that may have lost their popularity or been replaced by new ideas, may be worth recalling. 'Offers and catchers' is almost self-explanatory, with the catchers pursuing others until they touched them, at which time they had to join those who were already caught in a 'pen', which at school was the air raid shelter. The game finished when everyone was caught. 'Tracking' involved two teams as well; the first team setting off, armed with chalk to scribble arrows on the pavement or road for the 'trackers' to follow. There were no limits to this game and it was usually played through the streets. 'Hounds and hares' was a similar type of game.

Mallies were very popular and we had two games that were played regularly, 'dobbie' and 'sirey'. In 'dobbie' the marbles, or lemonade corks, if that was what you had, were placed in a small circle, and with the use of a 'dobber', which was either a large steel ball bearing or a ball made out of lead, you tried to knock the marbles out of the circle. If you missed you let your opponent in, but when you resumed playing you went from where the 'dobber' last finished. In 'sirey' you worked from a fixed distance to knock the marbles off a 'sire' or metal drain cover. In both games you kept what you dislodged. It was all very scientific and taken very seriously. After a successful day you went home with a pocketful of marbles or corks which you would probably lose the following day.

Ball games ranged from simple ones like 'donkey', which is still played, to more complicated ones like 'plainy, clappie, rolly, tobaccy', which involved throwing the ball up against a wall and performing a series of fixed contortions in between each throw. If you did not succeed in catching the ball before it hit the ground at any stage, you went back to the beginning. This was mostly played by girls. One particular skipping game, which I vaguely remember, was played to a chant that began: 'A cradle, a ladle, a piss pot, a pan,' which ran into several verses. It was also a girls' game. Boys were never that uncouth.

Most games required a selection process to pick teams, or to decide who ' had it on' in things like hide-and-seek. This was sorted out by saying a 'secret', normally a rhyme, at the end of which one person was eliminated. Some that come to mind are:

One potato, two potatoes, three potatoes, four,
Five potatoes, six potatoes, seven potatoes, more.

Eenie, meanie, miny mo
Catch a 'nigger' by the toe
If he squeals, let him go
Eenie, meanie, miny mo.

Or a very sophisticated variation that went:

Eenie meanie, miny mo
Set the baby on the po
When it's done
Wipe its bum
Eenie meanie miny mo.

Two others were:

Eetle ottle black bottle
Eetle ottle out
Tea and sugar is my delight
Tea and sugar is out.

Eachy, peachy, peary, plum
Throwing tatties up the lum
Santa Claus got one on the bum
Eachy, peachy, peary, plum.

There were others, equally delightful, and probably some of them are still in use. Something that was not a sport or a game but took hours of practice, and even then some never mastered it, was the two-fingered whistle, in all its various forms. The louder the better, of course, and it was often used to gain attention or bring a game to an end. All through life it can be a very valuable 'tool'.

Not all play was around the home or in its immediate vicinity. Beaches and other well-known play areas were used regularly. Moving out of town we had our own 'swimming pool', a small triangle of sand among the seaweed just below the coastguard station. Earlier swimmers had sunk three tar drums there and filled them with stones. These were our diving platforms, but only when tidal conditions were right. They were no use if they were too deeply submerged, or if there were only a few inches of water round the base. They had been set at selected places so that they came into use at different tides, and they remained there for many years before finally disintegrating with rust.

Further out, the Burn o' Weyland offered a little more in the way of sand, and it was more popular with families who had smaller children. The undulations in the banks along this part gave a certain amount of shelter and made the area ideal for picnics. On occasions, when time and distance were forgotten, we would wander along the beach as far as Carness, or across the fields to the bay between Carness and the Head of Work. There were some great bathing areas round there.

The next shore of note, going north-east, was the Bay of Meil. It was mined early in the war, presumably considered to be the only place the Germans would land if they decided to invade. Tragically, two young lads, Jimmy Fox and Tommy Kelday, were killed there when a group of pals tried to cross it. Apparently they were almost all across when one of them stepped on a mine. There was also a sailor killed in this area while out trapping rabbits. Needless to say, this beach never regained its popularity after the war. Further east, the Bay of Berstane with its slipway was

Scapa beach

another place for beach activities, and it was common practice to wander on round the point to the sands at Inganess Bay. There, the shipwrecked tanker lying not far offshore added a bit of variety as something to swim out to, climb over and dive off.

The only two remaining beaches within easy reach were Hatston, which was out of bounds during the war, as it had been developed as an aerodrome, and the lovely sandy stretch at Scapa. The drawback with Scapa was that it was a fair old hike from downtown Kirkwall. Bikes were not all that plentiful but what we had we shared. The system in vogue was that two set off on a bike, one on the crossbar, and two others started walking. After some distance the first two dismounted, laid the bike in the ditch, and then they started walking. When the second pair reached the bike, they mounted and cycled some distance past the walkers, before they in turn set it down. All four got there with only one bike, but no one had to walk more than half the distance. At Scapa there was often the bonus of seeing the fleet in, or finding a sailor's cap that had been washed ashore.

The old stone quarries at the top of East Hill and the nearby *whins* were great playgrounds, ideal for cowboys and indians and other 'warlike' games. Robin Hoods and Zorros could be seen sword fighting, firing arrows from bamboo bows and launching spears all over these areas. There was also a rifle range there, used by the army and the home guard. Occasionally, we were allowed to have a shot with a rifle by someone we knew.

The inherent dangers of the quarry itself were tragically brought home to us when we witnessed one of our schoolmates, Arthur Bews, drowning. He had been catching *brandies*, a favourite pastime with children of the time, when he fell in. We ran to the nearby farmhouse for help but all too late. It was a solemn warning, which was endorsed later when I too fell in, but was lucky enough to scramble back on to the bank with the help of Letty Firth. She took hold of me by the hair and hauled, while her brother Jimmy held on to her legs in case she too fell in. Had I been sporting a 'No 1' haircut, I probably would not be here to tell the tale.

Letty to the rescue

One of the more attractive 'playgrounds' of the time was the Peedie Sea. It was about twice its present size and also served as the local refuse dump. Filling it in began at the Pickaquoy side, working across to the Ayre Mills. All sorts of treasures could be found there, and you were never short of company as the whole area was alive with rats, particularly in the dark. On the other side of the road, just past where the Picky Centre is now, big Jock Newlands, locally known as Jock o' Picky, had a scrapyard. The main attraction there was the stack of empty tar drums, abandoned by council roadmen. The trick was to find two that had not been holed by a pick, which we could use to build a raft. It was amazing how stable they were, two drums fixed together with bits of scrap wood and rope. We paddled for miles through these murky waters. Attempts to rig up a sail were never very successful, and many a soaking we got in the stagnant, not very sweet-smelling water.

Many hours were spent just throwing stones - *dead man's plunges, skitheries* - or landing them on the 'Holmie', a small island now submerged under the Hydro power station. There was also an ample supply of bottles available to set up as targets. Stone throwing was almost an art form, where distance and accuracy blossomed with long practice. We also sailed boats, some proper models, but mostly made on the spot from scraps. Occasionally, the winter provided ice thick enough to skate on, or rather slide on, as skates were not too plentiful, but more often than not we went through the ice and got soaked. The water was not all that deep near the edges so there was never any real danger. The GPO telephone pole depot, where the bus station now stands, was also popular, with piles of poles stacked up ready for us to run, climb, or

Anchor's away

fall, over. All this area has been transformed. The only activity left on the Peedie Sea is model yacht sailing, but the Picky Centre makes up for some of what was lost.

Another 'wet' play area was the 'Ducky', where the Papdale Primary School now stands. Presumably, it was originally a duck pond but it had been developed into a proper yachting pond. It fell into disuse during the war, probably because most of the enthusiasts were away, and it gradually filled up with reeds. The hut that the yacht club owned had a window and we used to gaze longingly at the beautiful model yachts, up to six feet long, lying on racks. Later, I was lucky enough to have my own three feet boys' class model, made by my father, who had made several of those stored in the hut. One tale that goes along with the 'Ducky' concerned an elderly gentleman, who, apart from being an ardent sailing enthusiast, also suffered from St Vitus' Dance. Every year apparently, to the great delight of the kids, it was only a matter of time before excitement took over and he had to be fished out of the water by other sailing buffs. Orcadians have a tradition of laughing at adversity.

Further down, The Willows was a natural play area. It was a meeting place for our lot and the 'new houses' lot, mostly without hassle, but when a fight did occasionally break out between individuals rather than 'gangs', supporters became decidedly partisan.

The trees, rare in Kirkwall, were a big attraction. Climbing trees was as popular in Orkney as anywhere else when we had access to them. The advent of the latest Tarzan film always sparked off a rash of trapezes, and *peedie* Tarzans of all shapes and sizes yodelled and swung through the trees with great gusto. Actually, there was usually only one rope, or two at the most, sometimes quite long, hanging from a high branch, on which we swung spectacularly. Whoever put them up knew what they were doing. They had to find and get up to a suitable branch, high but strong and in a place where you could reach a launching pad on another tree. It was also essential that there were no other trees in your line of flight. Accidents were rare, as self-preservation seemed to strengthen the grip.

There was one particular trapeze, always erected in the same place over the burn, which

The Willows

caused a problem for the unwary. The drill there was to grab the rope, climb backwards up the slope on the road side as far as possible, then launch yourself out over the burn, letting go at a precise moment and landing safely on the opposite bank. That sort of precision was not always accomplished. An additional hazard for those not familiar with the set-up, was a branch stump just alongside where the rope was tied. Anyone who did not make it the first time and opted to swing back to gain further momentum, always got a shock and the inevitable soaking as the rope, as it always did, caught on this stump and let go again just as you were reaching mid-stream. The rope had to be cleared of this stump every time before setting out. Many a wet 'Tarzan' spent the afternoon in school after a lunchtime visit to The

Tarzan

Willows. The new trees planted by school pupils during the 1930s grew fast, and as they were very close together they provided ideal hiding and 'hunting' ground.

One of the spookier, but very popular, places to play was the Earl's Palace, especially in the *grimlings*; and, of course, being 'haunted', many a 'ghostly' footstep was heard there while playing hide-and-seek. It was more about nerve than finding a good hiding place. I guess it would make the hair curl yet.

The St Magnus kirkyard, just across the road, came into the same category but we did play there regularly until it became too dark for comfort. Some of us also used it as a short cut home from the BB hall, which stood on the site of the St Magnus Centre. There was an exit gate from the hall, which led on to the middle of Copland's Lane. From there, rather than take the Strynd route, we climbed over the kirkyard dyke and 'legged' it between the gravestones down to Broad Street. Alan Wells's 100 metre Olympic record must have been broken on many occasions by 12 and 14 year-olds in St Magnus kirkyard during the 1940s.

Earl's Palace

One 'playground' that has been mentioned a few times already, where I spent a lot of time, was Eastbank. It was almost a second home to me; not the hospital, I am glad to say, but the grounds and buildings around it. The house, which belonged to the hospital, was the home of the Firth family who were close friends of our family. Jim was the ambulance driver, but his responsibilities also included looking after the hospital garden; cutting all the grass throughout the fairly extensive grounds and keeping the furnace in the boiler house stoked, to ensure the hospital's hot water supply. He also 'fumigated' the hospital linen in the 'fectan' (disinfecting) shed and had many other duties. It was probably more than one man was capable of doing, and Vi, his wife, worked equally hard, helping with some of his chores, doing all her own work and bringing up five children. During the war, while Jim was in the army, Vi managed to keep things ticking over - apart from driving the ambulance, which she did not do - with some help from my folks, until he came out.

The Firth house was a great house to go to, and quite a few of us did regularly, including Mary and Christine Jolly, Moira Garden, Jim Robertson and some of the Sinclair boys from Viewforth. They had an amazing assortment of cats; 'Owie', 'Girnigow', 'Bonnyfit', 'Fumff' and 'Squek', to name but a few. They also kept hens.

I knew Jimmy, Letty and Rosie Firth best, as Alison and David were that bit younger. It is maybe just as well - it would have been a bit of a squeeze with seven of us in the bath on Friday nights. We had the whole hospital grounds to play in, more or less. We were warned to stay away from the 'fever' and TB wards, which we did to an extent, but we talked to patients, especially those with TB, who were encouraged to be out in the fresh air on nice days. It was not a disease that patients recovered from very often in those days and it was sad for us when someone we had got to know quite well died.

The grounds were surrounded by high dykes, as were the fields on Pat Turfus's farm next door. We walked miles along dyke tops; played in the large garden, helping ourselves to the odd strawberry, gooseberry or blackberry; climbed the trees and ran about in the park where the hens were kept. We erected swings on the trees and made see-saws from the pile of old timber at the top of the park. We did not go in the 'fectan' shed much as it smelt pretty strong at times, nor did we go in the drying shed, or the mortuary. On wet days we had the run of the house and the loft above the garage. We strayed as far as 'the *whins*' and the quarries just along the road, and often set off on bikes or on foot to some beach or other. We played 'hockey' in the hen park along with the grown ups, using old wooden-shafted golf clubs as sticks and a tennis ball. Many a 'black and blue' shin we got from that.

We also trapped rats, which were something of a pest round the hospital. Mostly, we used a wire cage with something tempting inside. When a rat went in, it could not get out, and we then took it to a water barrel and submerged the cage until the rat was dead. This was quite normal practice then, but I guess that it would be strongly disapproved of by animal rights groups today.

Eastbank had its share of visiting servicemen during the war and I remember one particular evening, as it was the first time either Jimmy or myself had tasted spirits. There was a navy rum ration standing on top of the table in the kitchen and we decided to find out how it tasted, so we picked up the 'halfie' and took a swig, neat. It was many a year before either of us tried it again.

Stories were all part of an evening at Eastbank, and one that amused me, told frequently by Jim, a great story-teller, was about Willie Harrison who worked at the auction mart. A stray and somewhat agitated *coo* had found its way into the grounds and had made its way up to the park above the house. Willie had ventured into this area with the intention of getting it cornered and eventually roped, but this particular animal made it very clear that it was in no mood to be captured. When it turned and Willie saw the look in its eye, he made for the nearest dyke. He was a man of advancing years

Willie's retreat

and not much over five feet 'tall', which made him considerably lower than the dyke, but Jim swore that he cleared the wall without touching it.

Chanties came into their own up at Eastbank, at least for me they did. Part of every household, they were not given much thought, certainly not by me until this particular one collapsed when I was sitting on it. What was strange was the fact that in this house in the centre of one of Orkney's major medical centres, Vi patched the *toot* up with brown gummed paper and Germoline. I have the scar yet. On another occasion, when Jimmy and Letty were both confined to bed with measles, I was visiting them - it was normal to put you in the way of these things, apparently to get them 'by with' - and in an attempt to cheer them up I was doing some 'acrobatics'. At one point I launched myself over their beds with the intention of landing on the floor at the other side - nothing if not ambitious. I only got about half way and disappeared down a gap between the beds, where the *chanty* was kept - exactly where it was kept. It took some time to get me dried off and sweet-smelling again, but at least I succeeded in cheering them up. I can't remember if I got the measles then or later.

Climbing and jumping off high dykes and other similar places was common practice. Cliffs were also great, and you soon learned the ones that were safe and those that weren't. Trees have been mentioned at The Willows, but Buttquoy, before the houses were built there, was also a good tree-climbing place. If the Tait family, who owned the park, minded, they never chased us off. Buildings were equally attractive, *shinning* up *spoots* or downpipes, then clambering up over the slates or tiles, to the ridge and, if available, down into the valley between. There were lots of options and Baikies' wood yard across from where we lived was excellent. Once up there you could make your way from West Castle Street over roofs and walls all the way to Burnmouth Road and back, without coming down. It gave you a feeling of power, looking down at people who could not see you. For some of the more adventurous, (or stupid may be a more accurate description), one particular dare, when you had been allowed up to the top of the Cathedral, was to climb out over the parapet and stand on one of the gargoyles while hanging on to the wall for grim death. Not one of the more sensible pastimes.

As I have mentioned, the many beaches available to us played a major part in our leisure activities. The hours we spent there were endless, just wandering along, usually with bare feet, wading in pools, turning over seaweed and stones to see what 'treasures' we could find. Sea life, in the form of crabs, *ersy crabs*, eels, *comper*s and other small fish, jellyfish, sea anemones, whelks, cockles, mussels, limpets and other shellfish, bits of coral, shells of all kinds, especially *grottiebuckies*, and more exotic things like *scarman's heads* and scallop shells, were there in abundance, just waiting to be 'discovered' and often as not carted home.

There were other things to be found, too; pieces of rope, buoys, bits of wood, even planks,

Happy days

Treasure seekers

Home time

blocks of candle wax, broken creels, sailors' caps, or whatever. There was stuff from the sea itself, some of it not too pleasant, such as dead seals, birds, basking sharks, even whales from time to time. As mentioned, the war produced its own 'collectibles' and other things that were better left alone. Wet feet, and worse, were inevitable, and if we had not taken them off, boots and shoes dried white with salt. Every stone or bunch of seaweed hid a potential 'treasure trove' and the expectancy never faded, particularly after a storm.

The variations in the shore can be quite striking. The favourite for the average city dweller on holiday is sand, sand and more sand, which we have in abundance. For those born near the sea, however, it is probably the least interesting aspect of the beach, unless there is a high percentage of shell sand where you can find *grottiebuckies*, pelicans' feet, tower shells, bubble shells, miniature *scarman's heads*, and others, to take home. Undoubtedly, for locals, the beaches covered in stones, boulders, rocks and seaweed in varying amounts and formations, are more attractive. Cliffs offer a different pastime, climbing along the base rather than up and down.

Having been brought up near a beach, we were scrambling along it almost as soon as we could walk and it gave us a certain amount of amusement watching city kids, either here on holiday or as refugees during the war, falling all over the place. It was a bit like watching Bambi on the ice. The yells that followed the appearance of a crab were a sure invitation to present one to them at every given opportunity. Some of them, but not all, got used to beachcombing after a time.

The smell of the seashore is basically a combination of various smells, some more dominant than others. There is the salty smell of the sea itself, seaweed fresh and rotting and fish at places where boats, creels and other equipment are stored; then there are the banks along the shore, with sea pinks, white clover, mint, dandelions, buttercups, thistles, grass and other wild plants. To an islander the rich aroma is unmistakable and very much part of home.

Whelks, cockles and *spoots* were hunted for in a more concentrated way, as they were part of our daily diet. Certain rocky shores were great for whelks; an acquired taste that we grew up with, happily winding them out of their shells with a pin and chewing them like sweeties - after they were boiled, of course. Gathering whelks was popular, partly for a treat to eat, but also to raise some extra pocket money by selling them to Meil's fish store. Harry Scollay, Davie Peace and I managed to acquire a second hand 'stop-me-and-buy-one' bike with which we expanded our potential in the whelk business. We eventually amassed the necessary £8 /15 shillings to send for an ex-army bell tent with a view to going camping. The future looked rosy. Unfortunately, the North of Scotland Shipping Company managed to lose it en route, so we ended up with no tent, and since they did not reimburse us, with no money either. We never forgave them.

Whelks inc.

Cockles came into the same category, but instead of picking them off the rocks they had to be dug out of the sand. *Spoots*, obviously still very popular, were taken with a knife, unless you were expert enough to use the fingers only. Walking backwards, watching for the hole to appear as they submerged deeper into the sand as you passed over was the usual way, but the more experienced could spot the 'eye' while walking forwards and whip it out of the sand before it had a chance to move. They are very tasty, particularly when fried lightly along with a bit of onion.

As mentioned earlier, fishing *sillocks* or *cuithes* was a common practice. Those caught at the Corn Slip or off one of the large sewers along the shore were never eaten, for obvious reasons, but those caught off the rocks at the Head of Work, or other similar places where the water was clean, were all right. If you wanted a decent catch, however, you had to get hold of a boat and head for the edge of the tide somewhere.

We had a twelve foot dinghy beached on the banks below Work Farm, which they stored for us in one of their outhouses all winter. When we went to the *sillocks*, out in 'The String' between the Head of Work and Helliar Holm, there were usually three in the boat, one rowing, generally Dad, and two fishing. We used proper *wands* with a cast containing three hooks, which were baited and trailed over the stern of the boat. When you hit a shoal you were pulling them in three at a time. It was a great thrill, that sudden tugging on the end of the line, and you knew you were in for a busy time. In no time, the bottom of the boat was awash with wriggling and jumping fish. Going ashore a few hours later with several score, our first stop was Work Farm, where the Meil family made you most welcome. We all sat down to a supper of fried *sillocks* or *cuithes* with *bere bannocks* and farm butter, and a glass of milk or *home-brew*. A second fry up was expected at home, often after having handed in a supper to a neighbour or friend. This generosity was partly due to the fact that *sillocks*, being grey fish, were not all that wonderful the following day.

On one slightly less happy occasion, I fell off my bike on the way to Work, and later when I began to feel sick on the boat I was 'landed' in semi-darkness at the outermost point of the Head of Work. From there I tramped for what seemed to be miles over the heather and bog back to the farm and then cycled home. It was a bit eerie out there.

Pooties were treated in the same way as *sillock*s but they were not quite as plentiful. Setting skate lines behind Helliar Holm was another great day out. The results could be disappointing and a whole day wasted if, as happened occasionally, a shoal of dogfish came along and that was all you got. They were not eaten. Trout fishing was popular enough but it was not something I tried until much older. I prefer them coming in three at a time. *Brandies* were caught with a jar on the end of a piece of string. It was lowered into a freshwater pond or quarry and pulled up at regular intervals until a catch was made. They were taken home for pets, not for eating, but they rarely lasted more than one or two nights.

Crabs were caught off rocks or slipways by lowering a tempting piece of bait on a string and letting it fall between the toes of the selected crab. When he grabbed it you whipped him quickly but carefully out of the water, before he realised what was happening. We gathered them in a bucket and eventually, when it was time to go home, they were counted and then thrown back in.

Another outdoor activity was hunting for wild birds' nests and eggs. We tramped the hills and

Night at the 'sillocks'

cliff tops in search of nests made by *teeicks*, whaups, *dunters*, plovers, etc, and if there were eggs, they were tested in water to see if they were *sitten*. If they sank they were all right and taken home for the table, but if they floated end up they were returned carefully to the nest to hatch.

Referred to already, a major pastime was swimming. The Orkney climate does not lend itself to swimming outside, but with no alternative available it was the sea or nothing. We swam all summer even from as early as March on one occasion, when Johno Moodie, Beetle and myself decided to take the plunge in Kirkwall Harbour. Needless to say we did not stay in long. I have mentioned the various beaches available to us, and there was also the pier at Scapa, which was cleaner. If you could swim, however, *the Basin* was the place to go - it had everything apart from clean water. We ignored the various things that floated; oil, tins, bottles and others that we won't mention. It mostly gathered in corners, so after a short run you took a big jump or dive, making a huge splash, which scattered a lot of it, and you did not re-surface until well clear. Where we went was decided according to the direction of the wind, the space left by boats and the availability of a suitable boat to dive from. The pier was not nearly high enough. A degree of caution was necessary if swimming off *the openings* or one of the many iron ladders attached to the pier at low tide. It was not always possible to reach them from the sea to pull yourself out and it was a fair swim to reach *the Corny* or the beach. As many as twenty or more went in on a good day. Most of us rarely stayed in more than half an hour until the teeth started chattering, but some seemed to be able to stick it for much longer.

Changing places were plentiful, with boxes, crates, sacks, horseboxes, creels and what-have-you all over the place. Modesty was not something that bothered us all that much but we tried to use a little decorum.

New swimmers started at the Corn Slip. There were always lobster boxes anchored fairly close to the slipway, and the drill was to dive or jump in, thrash about in the general direction of a box and grab the edge before going under. You then climbed aboard, and, after plucking up courage, again leapt in, reaching dry land with a few more frantic strokes. As confidence grew, you targeted a small boat a bit further out, and in no time at all you were swimming the full length of *the Basin*.

Takin' spoots

The BB's did the tests for their swimming badges and certificates there, swimming galas were held, and later when the junior inter-counties began, the swimming races also took place in the harbour.

Winter brought its own fun. Snow was a big thing with us, a really big thing. The first signs always brought smiles to our faces. Looking out through the classroom window watching huge snowflakes drifting down, silhouetted against the sky, put all thoughts of lessons out of the head. New, soft snow was usually best for snowballs but for sledging it had to be packed by vehicles, maybe thaw a little and then freeze hard. At school during break times, groups got together to 'raise' a slide by following each other down the same strip of hard packed snow, usually on a slope, and continuing until it was sheer black ice. Then it was ready for going flat out, doing *hookeries*, sliding one-legged, or forming a chain, one behind the other, upright or on *hookers*. The end depended on where the slide was raised, and it tended to get longer with use, but crashing into a wall or railing at the finish all added to the thrill. Rubber boots were no use, and shoes or boots with protectors were severely discouraged as they cut up the surface. Bumps and wet behinds were all part of it, as were 'picked' knees.

Snowball throwing sometimes led to a snowball fight with groups taking sides and pelting one another. If made from new powdery snow, the snowballs were soft, or packed almost rock hard when made from wet snow. Unless you were unlucky enough to get one in the eye, little harm was done. Another option was to try and throw one over the science room roof from the front of the boys' shelters at the lower end of the playground. Windows were in some danger but I don't remember one ever getting broken. One lad, who was particularly good both for distance and accuracy, was Norman Smith. He was the son of a lighthouse keeper, and as such, spent a lot of his spare time at the beach throwing stones. His technique was excellent. We were not aback of throwing snowballs at grown-ups as well; even the odd teacher or policeman became a target provided you knew them really well, but mostly we took the precaution of doing it from a place of concealment. We weren't all that brave.

As mentioned, some did skating, but ponds and lochs rarely froze over hard enough to take a chance. The ice was too thin. Skates were in short supply and 'clogs' were more popular, which were shaped in wood with metal runners and usually made at home. They were used on roads, downhill, much in the way that roller blades are now. Skiing was done, but very little. The only people I remember with skis were Bruce Dunnet and Alfie Walls, who made their own skis at school. We were warned not to eat snow or suck icicles, as they would give us impetigo. Snowmen and igloos were built, but not very often. We preferred more active fun.

The real snow sport for us, which illustrates one of the big changes between then and now, was sledging. With hardly any cars or lorries about, especially in the evenings, we had the main roads virtually to ourselves. We were spoiled for choice but choose we did, purely on the grounds of which hill was in the best condition. The 'Eastie' was very well used. You could start from the gate at Viewforth, or better still from Bob Garden's house, Noltland. It was the longer run but the real attraction was 'Crystal's Corner' where Berstane Road meets East Road. Negotiating that particular bend at full lick, when the conditions were icy, was great. Clay Loan was really fast, even slightly dangerous, but in good conditions you got a superb run right down to Junction Road. The Holm Branch was also used if the Kirkwall roads were too cut up, but we preferred to stay in town.

The real 'king pin', however, was Dundas Crescent. From 'the gun' in front of Warrenfield you got a fabulous run all the way down to the junction of Palace Road and School Place - no traffic island then - where you had a choice. You could either veer left towards Broad Street or keep straight on down to the top of The Strynd. It was heady stuff, the only drawback being the good half mile walk back up again, pulling your sledge behind you, which we happily kept doing until it was time to go home.

During the war the only light available was moonlight, if there was a moon, which was reflected by the snow. Sledges varied quite a bit in size from small, 'single-seater' ones to the big ones that held up to five or six people. The big ones, through sheer weight, went faster and were steered in one of two ways. In the first, the pilot sat in front with a skate attached to one foot, and the sledge virtually followed the direction chosen by the skate. The second method was to have a second, smaller sledge behind the big one on which the steersman lay flat on his stomach, peering down one side and man-handling it in what ever direction he wanted it to go. I say he, because girls were never allowed to take on this responsibility. Everyone had to keep their feet tucked well in and on no account touch the ground, which would spray hard snow in the steersman's face. Some big sledges had wooden levers on either side, which were dug into the snow to alter course, but they were never very successful. Small sledges were invariably steered by lying flat on the stomach and digging in one toe or the other to control direction.

Sledging

Sledges were mostly home-made, with the running boards on the bigger ones made very strong to take the immense pressure when turning a corner, or especially when 'broadsiding' at the end. I remember 'Bricky' Bews having a proper toboggan, but they were not common. There was a sort of status symbol in having a flashy sledge, and the 'Red Devil' owned by Dave Peace was one that springs to mind. The first sign of snow initiated the unearthing of the sledge from a shed or attic, and the runners were prepared by rubbing them with a file or sandpaper to get the rust off and then finished off with handfuls of snow to make them shine. Then you were ready. Roads were not salted or gritted until the traffic in Kirkwall increased enough to merit it, but that was much later.

Accidents did happen, of course. I remember the night Kenny Wards broke his ankle while he was acting as steersman, with a skate in front of a big sledge. It ran into the gable end of the house that faces up East Road and his foot was between the sledge and the wall when it hit. There were other similar injuries, but the only fatality I knew of was a 'Wren' during the war. She and her sailor boyfriend persuaded one of the lads to let them have a shot of his sledge on Clay Loan. Unfortunately, they had no idea what they were doing and ran straight into the joiner shop that used to face up the Loan. He fell off just before they crashed and survived, but she was killed. It taught us a lesson never to lend our sledges to strangers again. The only safeguard on offer was the occasional load of sand spread at the bottom of a hill by workmen from Kirkwall Town Council. To be honest, we preferred it without since it did away with the added thrill of a 'broadside' at the bottom. Very occasionally, Bob Craigie or one of the other policemen would be delegated to come and keep control - not to stop us, but just to make sure that everything was in order, although I don't think their hearts were in it. They would sooner have joined in.

When a rare car hoved in sight everyone started shouting 'MCC' ('motor car coming') and sledges were pulled into the side before reaching the 'danger' area. Cars with chains on their wheels were not popular as they cut up the surface, and they were soundly pelted with snowballs all the way up. We knew most of them anyhow; Bob Garden, John Jolly, Dr Marwick and others, who lived up the hill, and to be fair they did not use it unnecessarily. They were only trying to get home, but that did not stop them from being severely snowballed and 'verbally abused'.

Clearly this activity is no longer possible, which is a pity. It was one of the best forms of entertainment we had and quite a few older 'boys' enjoyed it just as much as we did. Of course, knees and other bare bits were 'picked' by the constant dampness and hard frosts. Cracked lips were also a nuisance, and it took days for them to heal as they kept re-opening with further frosts. Nail cold was another painful thing, the result of hours of throwing snowballs. Firstly your fingers went numb, and then, as the feeling started to come back, the pain under the nails was excruciating, followed finally by severe itching.

At the end of the day, weary but sitting cosy and warm in front of a blazing coal fire, nail cold gone, knees and lips soothed with Snowfire and sipping a hot drink while looking at the pictures drawn by Jack Frost on the window panes, all your aches and pains soon disappeared.

(Perhaps 'global warming' has been going on longer than we think. I imagine that we had far more snow then than we have now, but then I imagine we had many more sunny days as well!)

Indoor games were sometimes active but more often passive in nature. The more robust games like table tennis were played with limited movement on the kitchen table, but more usually in places like the Toc H, (later the community centre), where there was plenty of space. That is where the best of our table tennis players were to be found most evenings. Snooker was slightly more flexible. Again, there were excellent facilities in the Toc H, and in Costie's, the Masonic Lodge and the Orkney Club.

It was also possible to play snooker at home on a quarter or half size table. We had one that had a proper slate bed which had to be set up, levelled and ironed each time before playing. A regular event during the winter involved my father with three, sometimes four, friends, playing for high stakes. Each 'contestant' took in 20 cigarettes and the winner at the end of the evening kept the lot. One of the players, Jim Firth, also had a table at his home which was permanently set up in the loft above the ambulance garage. Snooker and the occasional glass of ale were enjoyed by the men, while the wives knitted and put the world to rights in the best room. I was allowed to keep score. I was also allowed to bring friends in to play and many a great session we had playing snooker, or darts, which was another popular game. Most of the homes we visited, both in Kirkwall and Shapinsay, had a dartboard, permanently hung up in one room or another, and several sets of darts. Apart from '301', we played quite a lot of 'Shanghai'. In this game you each threw a dart to get a number, then after getting the 'double' of your number you tried for the 'double' of each of the others, thus knocking them out. The last one to survive was the winner

Sometimes an evening of darts or snooker with schoolmates expanded into more robust activities such as cushion fights, and there was one particular occasion when a cushion burst, spraying feathers everywhere. I didn't think I had particularly tidy pals, but by the time my mum came home there was not a feather to be seen anywhere. The flat cushion, however, was a bit of a giveaway. The afore-mentioned 'Hacky' was involved in this affair, as he was one evening, after football, when we toasted every scrap of bread in the house for our supper. Breakfast the following morning was a bit sparse.

As we were too young to be members of the Orkney Club or the Masons, Costie's was where we played most of our snooker. It was one of the popular gathering places for teenage boys. Bill Costie, who owned the pavilion, encouraged us to come provided we behaved properly both on and off the tables. It paid him really, as the bulk of the snooker played there was by our age group. After school, between 4.30pm until it closed at 11pm, we gathered there in groups; not all at once and not every night, but frequently. We paired off and booked 30 minutes or an hour on one of the two tables. In between, we drank tea or Vimto, ate cakes or sweets, blethered and some smoked. Bill used to open a packet of cigarettes and sell them singly to those who could not afford any more. By this time I was working as a message boy and had money to spend. I was also fortunate in having some good 'moneyed' mates, 'Billo', 'Hacky' and others, who never saw me short. Even before a football match we would meet there first. We also played tennis on the two hard courts, hiring rackets and balls at the counter. In addition, there was a putting green of sorts. If you were looking for one of your pals, there was more than an even chance you would find him at Costie's sometime during the evening. Apart from playing tennis, girls did not go there.

Table or board games were also a regular part of our entertainment. Evenings at home were spent playing various card games such as 'Batchy', 'Euchre', 'Five Hundred', 'Snap', 'Spoof' (or 'Sevens'), 'Black Peter', 'Slippery Anne', 'Hearts', 'Rummy', and we gambled big time for matches, playing 'New market'. We also had the usual board games like 'Ludo', 'Snakes and ladders', 'Tiddlywinks', 'Monopoly' and some not seen now, such as 'Totopoly', a game based on horse racing, and 'Main Line', where the object was to construct railway tracks. 'Happy Families', 'Donkey', 'Lexicon', and other well-known card games were in most houses, and new 'war' games such as 'Spies' or 'Battleships' were popular, though we had to draw our own 'battlefields' on blank paper. We also had a 'Bagatelle' board where we rolled steel ball bearings round a sloping, figure eight shaped surface. The object was to catch the balls in a selection of 'pockets': the top half of the board counting for and the bottom half against.

Jigsaws were a big thing in our house, something that I still enjoy around Christmas, and all the family used to work at them. Games which were slightly more on the edge were 'Consequences' and one called 'Truths and dares', where you chose either to answer any question you were asked truthfully or you opted to fulfil any 'dare' that was put to you. Games played in the dark, such as 'Murderers' or 'Sardines', were regular features on evenings when there were quite large gatherings of family or friends. 'Sardines' depended on everyone understanding the rules, otherwise it was possible to have two or more groups all hiding from one another in separate places at the same time. 'Murderers' could be creepy, particularly for younger kids, when the person who was being 'strangled' might let out a most horrendous scream.

Other games, or more accurately challenges, involved broom handles or chairs. One consisted of setting the end of a broom on the floor up against the skirting board, then trying to ease your whole body under it from one side to the other with only your feet touching the floor. Another involved starting with the broom handle held in both hands behind your back, bringing it up over your head, down the front, stepping through it and ending up with it back where you started, all without letting go with either hand. Strength contests were carried out by two lads facing one another with both hands clasped round the broom handle and held above the head. The test was to bring it down to waist level, keeping the arms straight, to see whose grip gave way. Another was to lift a dining room chair off the floor, keeping it level with only one hand holding the bottom of either front leg. Still another was to stand behind a chair, take hold of the back at the top with both hands, raise it to chin level, then twist the chair bodily until the legs were pointing horizontally out in front, then you straightened your arms. A balancing feat was to set a chair on its front legs with the back parallel to the ground. You placed your knees on the back legs and grasped the top with your hands. A matchbox was placed just in front. The test of balance was to lean forward, easing the top down to the floor, bend forward without falling and pick up the matchbox with your teeth before restoring the chair to its original position. It was hard going and hard on chairs - not recommended for antiques. Handstands, somersaults, forward or backward, 'crab' walking, along with other acrobatic pursuits were also well practised. Boxing and wrestling were always popular and the boxing continued for some of us up into the Kirkwall Athletic Club and even Johnny Smith's boxing booth at the market. Apart from Henry Cooper, 'Keaton' Johnston, from our street, had the wickedest left hook I ever saw.

Another use for a chair

Toys were different in the 1930s and '40s. There was a shortage of metal, required for the 'war effort', and plastic was not yet invented, but we still had toys. Girls probably played more with dolls than they do now. They were made of porcelain or cloth, the former having to be handled reasonably carefully or it would break. Dolls' clothes were made at home. Wooden toys for boys were the more common thing and having a dad with a good pair of hands, I was never short. I had a large red 'tipper' lorry, scale models of a destroyer and an Air Sea Rescue launch, both of which could sail, and, as mentioned earlier, I also had a boys' class model yacht with two sets of sails made of parachute cloth. I still have it, but the sails need replacing. Things like stilts, scooters, swords, bows, arrows, spears and other items were regularly produced when time allowed.

We also made kites out of a piece of spare cloth, two sticks, a bit of string and some paper to make the tail, but in truth they never flew very well. We made *plushneys* out of strips of rubber cut from an inner tube, a piece of stiff fencing wire and a bit of leather to hold the stone. Slings were made out of strong string and a piece of leather. We also made a thing that had been a toy for many generations, known as a *snorry bone*. All it consisted of was a small bone from a pig's foot, about three inches long with a bulge at each end, and a piece of string tied in a loop at the centre, creating a handle on each side. It was then *wupped* around until tight, the strings were pulled, and the bone began to spin at a furious rate, making a loud snoring noise.

On a lesser scale we made paper aeroplanes, or bought a cheap glider made from card with a lead nosepiece and a piece of elastic to launch it. Something that cost nothing was an old tyre, the bigger the better, which we propelled at great speed with stick or hand, especially downhill. There are too many cars around now for this kind of activity.

Snorry bone

One thing, which was hardly a toy, but was very much treasured if you happened to possess one, was a sheath-knife. It was usually worn with pride, housed in a sheath attached to your trouser belt. It was kept sharp for paring wood, peeling *neeps* and other necessities, and often thrown at barn or byre doors to see if you could make it stick. It was never considered to be a dangerous 'toy'.

More constructive toys included Meccano sets. The pieces were made of metal, some getting a bit rusty if the set had been used a lot. By following the instruction booklet it was possible to make anything from a crane to a train. Spare nuts and bolts could be bought at Leonards. Frustration could creep in if you found you were one piece or a few nuts and bolts short to complete what you were making. Meccano sets varied in size and I was lucky enough to have a big one, given to me by Hamish Flett and his brother David, which they had outgrown. Many happy hours were spent with it, often with friends, and eventually it was passed on to my nephew many years later.

There were other excellent play-things in our house. There was a magic lantern, which we got from old John Copland, with a collection of coloured 3" x 3" slides depicting the story of Robinson Crusoe. We spent many happy hours in a darkened box room with this lantern.

There were two very special presents. The first one was a 'Diana' air rifle, complete with targets, darts and a box of lead slugs. I got it from 'Santa', when I was eight. It gave endless enjoyment, and in time I improved as a shot. Unfortunately, it also gave me the courage to wreak revenge on a certain massive female dragon who lived across the street and not only put the fear of death in the kids, but most of the parents as well. From our upstairs window I shot her in the backside with a slug. I could hardly miss. From that distance, however, and the fact she would assuredly have been protected by a pair of whalebone corsets and several layers of clothing, the pain would not have been much - but it did make her jump. Mercifully, she didn't figure out what had happened or I would have been in deep trouble. My folk never found out either, or that would have been the end of my shooting days. That was my only attempt at 'big game hunting' and clearly, with the wisdom of hindsight and the sense of responsibility that comes with being a grandfather, I know that what I did was wrong, but at the time I felt as Montgomery must have felt; that I was making a strike for freedom and justice.

The other present of special importance was my first bike, a boys' size one. It was no great shakes when I saw it first but my father stripped it right down, black-enamelled it, fitted new brake shoes, pedal blocks, hand grips and whatever else it needed. It was the most beautiful thing I had ever seen and first day out I was 'cock o' the walk'. Unfortunately, the first day did not end that way. While cycling out the 'Munt' road, with Ian Sinclair on the crossbar, I collided with the black wooden railings next to the shore and buckled the pedal so badly it wouldn't turn. Despair turned to joy a few days later when it was again restored to its pristine condition, and Ian Sinclair got good leave to walk after that - for a time at least.

Six years later, I bought my first new bike - a full-size Rudge Whitworth, complete with three speed gears - from Alfie Walls, for the princely sum of £12. It was the only other bike I ever had and many a mile we travelled both for work and pleasure. It had a rough end to its long career as transport for timber, plasterboard, and whatever else was needed for building our house at Pipersquoy Road in Kirkwall. It must have carried literally tons of building materials over its last few years. It was with some regret that I finally decided to put it to the local dump, but I was equally delighted, as I left, to see a small lad picking it up and heading home with it. I hope it gave him as many happy hours as it gave me.

Bikes were an important part of our entertainment and looking after them was something we learned to do; oiling, tightening and greasing the chain, replacing brake-blocks and mending punctures. Punctures, even in tyres with little more than the canvas left, were mended with John Bull outfits. We removed the tyre using spoons as levers, found the hole by submerging the tube in water, cleaned the area round it with a matchbox making sure it was dry before spreading the 'solution'. When the solution was almost dry a suitable patch was pressed on and French chalk sprinkled round the area to stop the tube from sticking to the tyre. Testing the valve with a drop of spittle was vital before the tyre was pronounced sound again. Lights were a bit of a novelty at first, but as they had to have new batteries and bulbs on a regular basis they were soon forgotten.

Brakes were considered to be important. Brake blocks, however, did not last long and eventually we gave up replacing them and developed our own braking system. One method was to hook your foot round the front of the handlebars and press the mudguard down on to the tyre. This was fine for gentle braking but it was not enough on a steep hill. It also had the drawback of making you somewhat unstable. Jamming the toe of your shoe in between the forks and the rear wheel worked much better. The harder you pushed the more you braked. You could even lock the wheel and do a 'skid'. It was a technique learned by trial and error. One lad who stayed across the street from us was introduced to this during the time he and his brother spent in Orkney as refugees from Edinburgh (because of the war not just because of Edinburgh). On his first attempt on my bike on 'the Eastie', he panicked, overdid the pressure, and lost most of the sole off one of his brand new sandals - bought of course, with a fair chunk of his clothing allowance. He was not a happy bunny. City kids have a lot to learn when they move out of town. There's more to being a 'country yokel' than having straw in your hair and *sharn* on your boots.

Some bikes had back pedal brakes and others had a fixed wheel. When you had a fixed wheel you could not stop pedalling no matter how fast the bike was going, which made life very difficult when going down a steep hill. Your legs either had to go like a windmill in a gale or you took your feet off the pedals altogether. Some places you went to had no children's bikes and as you could not reach the seat, you had to learn to cycle with your body out to one side and a leg pushed through under the crossbar to reach the other pedal.

We made carts out of scrap timber and old pram wheels, which we rode down 'the Eastie' and other suitable hills. Again, braking was a problem, and it usually ended up with damaged shoes or leaping off when things got out of hand.

Hobbies cover a lot of activities; anything from gathering and pressing wild flowers to woodwork. Parents' hobbies often filtered down to the children and woodwork was certainly something in our family, after three generations of joiners. Model making, dolls' houses and cribs, fretwork, French polishing; anything and everything to do with wood was done in our house. When I went up to Baikie's joiner shop across the road, tools and wood were always available to work with, even from a fairly early age. Some of the joiners who worked there through the war, like Alfie Flett, Johnny Morrison and Johnny Kirkness, had their own businesses, but, because their work force had been called up to the services, they joined the staff of Baikie's for the duration. They all helped if you were stuck. Woodwork continued as you got into the 'big' school and also in the BB woodwork class, both under the teaching of Alfie Harcus. The school had a limited amount of timber available and a mistake while cutting from a sheet of plywood could be a minor disaster, and something you were not allowed to forget.

Girls tended to concentrate on sewing, embroidery, crochet, knitting and other needlecrafts. Another craft that was useful as well as fun was knotting and splicing, using bits of rope or heavy string. We could splice, back splice, tie 'sheep shanks', 'bowlines', 'running bowlines', reefs, etc; all handy but, unfortunately, much of it forgotten now. Making bracelets from coloured plastic wire, bought by the yard from Pat Sutherland's, was another popular phase. We modelled things out of 'plasticine' and 'glitter wax', made candles out of blocks of candle wax which had been washed up on the beach in Shapinsay, and we cast anchors out of molten lead. The accent invariably was on making and creating.

Another interest was collecting. Almost anything was collected; silk flags and flowers from cigarette packets, matchboxes, coins, stamps, and, of course, badges and other 'war' items. A certain amount of 'horse-trading' went on amongst us to try and improve our collections.

Scrapbooks were also enjoyable. My sister had a big one in which she stuck pictures of the Royal Family, particularly the two princesses, Elizabeth and Margaret. I collected football pictures, mostly from newspapers, and had a valuable source of supply when I worked for WHB Sutherland. He saved his weekly papers for me, and I picked them up every Saturday morning when I delivered the messages.

Drawing, not painting, was a favourite pastime; horses and people mostly, but anything that took the fancy. The choice of hobbies was wide and most of us found something that interested us.

A dressing up box or trunk containing old clothes, sometimes from a couple of generations back and nearly always female, was common in most homes. Many a happy hour was spent dressing up, mostly by girls, especially if a pair of high-heeled shoes could be found to stagger around in. Music was also very important in our lives and, as mentioned earlier, 'sing-songs' were a regular feature. Less active evenings were spent sitting with the lights out looking for pictures in the coal fire, or making shadows on the ceiling, accompanied by the comforting singing of a kettle on the hob. There was probably more incentive and scope for the imagination then with no TV, videos, hi-fi, Gameboys and fewer toys to occupy active minds.

Pets were a big thing in most houses, but not in ours. We had goldfish - not the most exciting or communicative pets to have. We did have various cats for short spells. My sister had a kitten which fell asleep under Bill Reid's lorry and that was the end of it. I had a black and white kitten called 'Scamp' that 'mysteriously' got out one night and never came back. Two other kittens, 'Korky' and 'Peter' were 'transported' to Shapinsay after digging in a neighbour's flowerbed. At least we saw them when we were there on holiday.

We also had a budgie, 'Charlie', who was very well treated with cuttlefish, *rattin tails*, chickweed and other delicacies, but even after talking to him for hours, he never said one word, as we had been assured he would. We had a canary which was frequently let out into the room to stretch his wings. On one occasion, his last, my mum spotted an open window to which it was heading and managed to slam it shut. Unfortunately, the canary was just passing through at the time, and half of it escaped, while the other half decided to stay at home. Two pigeons were in my possession for only a few hours. I had managed to 'acquire' the necessary two shillings to purchase two 'homing' pigeons from a mate, but unfortunately they escaped and I never saw them again - at least I don't think I did. The two shillings had to be paid for, of course, by the inevitable *skelped erse*. A stray collie also became mine for a few hours, offered to me by Jim Couper who was driving the steamroller at the time. He fixed me up with a length of rope, at least 30 yards of it, to take the dog home. I was over the moon but unfortunately it too 'escaped' while I was in looking for something for it to eat. We had no other pets as far as I can remember.

Picnics were always welcome. They were rarely planned in advance - the weather usually put paid to that - but when the decision was made to go, a picnic hamper was not long in appearing, and off we went. Usually, we went on foot, but sometimes if we were going a fair distance, bikes were shared to speed things up, and on rare occasions we were transported there in relays, on Jim Firth's motor bike and sidecar. Scapa, Berstane, Work, Carness, the Burn o' Weyland, even the golf course, which was not used on a Sunday, were favourites. 'Golfies', found on the course were very valuable, and even if in poor shape they could still have the cover taken off and all the elastic unwound.

Beaches, however, were the more attractive option, as there was plenty to do when you got there, and organised games with everybody joining in were the best. The picnic itself was devoured with relish; loads of home bakes, along with milk or lemonade, or tea made on a primus stove, or sometimes on a small bonfire. Occasionally, large family groups would hire a bus and set off to some attractive spot for a day out. There were also official picnics organised by the Co-op or the Sunday schools, etc.

Reading was another very important thing in our spare time. We always had comics, most of which came on alternate weeks. Early ones, still popular though the characters have mostly changed, were *The Beano* and *The Dandy*, but there were others probably long since defunct such as *The Knockout, Radio Fun* and *The Magic*. For older boys there was *The Hotspur, Wizard, The Adventure* and *The Rover*. They contained stories or serials featuring such sporting heroes as the 'Cannonball Kid', the best centre forward that ever was, and 'Handy Andy', with enormous hands and feet, seen to be very clumsy until he dived into the water where he swam like a fish. Then there was the athlete 'Wilson', whose age no one knew, but even though he would certainly have been drawing the pension, he was still unbeatable in almost any length of race. There was 'Sexton Blake' the detective, and one of the really popular ones, 'Wild Young Dirkie', a young Highlander, who could knock the eye out of a bluebottle from thirty yards with one of the many 'dirks' he carried in his belt. I even braved putting on my sister's kilt and raced around 'the mountains' eliminating hundreds of English soldiers. My daughter Karen, who heard this story, not from me that's for sure, still refers to me as 'Wild Young Birkie', which was probably nearer the truth.

Libraries were the main source of reading material. The Navy had taken over the upstairs area of the Kirkwall Free Library in Laing Street as an officers' club in 1940, which was deemed to be more important than the museum which had been housed there. The museum collection was put into storage for the duration of the war, and did not resurface until Tankerness House Museum came into being (now re-named the Orkney Museum). Library provision was basic. All there was in the way of books was in one room. When you entered, you were confronted by the desk; a high pulpit-like structure made out of Japanese oak, where Mr Flett the custodian stood, looking formidable, on the raised floor. You handed your books up before going through a gate on the left, into the area where the books were shelved. We went to the children's section, looking for the latest *Just William, Billy Bunter*, or whatever else we fancied. When ready to go, you again approached the desk on the opposite side, passed your books up to be date-stamped before escaping through another gate and then out on to the street. If you spoke at all it was in whispers, or you were likely to get a rocket, but loud enough to be heard above the librarian, who whistled continuously through his teeth.

On the left of the entrance you passed through a door in a glass partition into the Reading Room, which had two large tables and papers and magazines available to browse through. A small room off this area was the committee room, used for meetings by local football clubs, trade unions and other groups. That was the sum total of library provision at that time.

Sometimes we spoke of 'the Albert' but mostly we went to 'the pictures' or 'the flicks', which probably referred to the silent films with their flickering pictures - before my time! It was superb entertainment, and most Saturday afternoon matinées were filled with hordes of noisy bairns. Dougie Shearer was a patient man, and in spite of the hassle and noise we created, I cannot ever remember seeing Dougie wigging anyone off. He did have a 'bouncer' of sorts, Mr Cook, who patrolled the aisle regularly with his torch. One flash and you quickly settled down, otherwise you were liable to be ejected.

The arrangement inside consisted of a number of rows of wooden seats, covered in rexine, down at the front, which we reached by a side passage. There was a wooden 'barrier' behind us, separating us from the red 'plush' seats, which occupied about half the total seating area, and finally, there were blue 'plush' seats at the back for those who had reservations. The dearer seats were approached by a central stairway. Nine pence, in old money, was the cheapest entrance fee that I remember, and it progressed to 1/6d for the red seats and 2/- for the blue. As soon as the lights went out there was always a lot of activity, the bolder lads sneaking under the barrier to get a *comfy* seat. It was hardly worth the effort, as Mr Cook was an expert at spotting ten-year-olds with 9d tickets planted in red plush seats, especially if they were the only ones there. For some reason, the plush seats always seemed to fill up from the back, leaving us high and dry - can't think why.

Another regular ploy was for someone to go to the 'loo' behind the screen, which had a fire door out into the lane. One boy went in and when the coast was clear, five came out. Dougie quietly turned a blind eye to all this, knowing that we would have had a struggle to raise the money for even one of us to get in.

We sat patiently through the Pathé News, enjoyed Donald Duck or Popeye, followed sometimes by a documentary in the *March of Time* series, before settling down to the main feature. We had our idols; James Cagney, Spencer Tracey, Mickey Rooney, Roy Rogers, The Lone Ranger and Tonto, Flash Gordon, Johnny Weismuller, and the funny men Abbot and Costello, Laurel and Hardy, and, of course, the prince of them all, Charlie Chaplin. Tarzan and cowboy films were the favourites and we all cheered when the cavalry arrived, or when Johnny Weismuller came to the rescue swinging through the trees. We played at being Billy the Kid, the Sisco Kid, the Oklahoma Kid, Tarzan and what-have-you, for days after each film. Before Disney films came along, most of the films were in black and white. We had some great 'movies'; *Captains Courageous*, *Boys' Town*, both with Spencer Tracey; the original *Jungle Book*, with Mowglie the starring character; *Shane* and *Winchester 73*, two of the great westerns, and, later, the early war stories were very popular. Of course, there were films like *The Werewolf*, which could be a bit too much for some and an early exit was the order of the day. Even the 'witchy' bits in *The Wizard of Oz* or *Snow White*, took a bit of coping with.

It was difficult to get in sometimes if the film was particularly well-known, and there were occasions when you suffered the disappointment of being turned away. Queues went all the way down to the bottom of the lane alongside the cinema and when you had to join the queue past a certain point you knew your chances were slim. There were always 'queue jumpers' of course and 'aggro' often occurred when someone joined a friend half-way up the queue.

When the show finished, as soon as 'The End' appeared on the screen, there was a mad stampede for the exits to try and escape before the National Anthem was played. If we did not make it, like true patriots we shot to attention (more or less) until it was completed. During the war we had an alternative venue, the Naval Cinema, where the Arts Theatre is now, but it was never as nice.

It all ended in 1947, after about 20 years of showing great films, when the Albert went on fire. In spite of valiant efforts by the firemen and various volunteers, including some of us children (delighted to miss an hour or so of school), the place was totally destroyed and never

CONCERT PARTY c. 1945/46
Back row: Self; John Flett; Evan Macgillivray; Colin Macgillivray; Jim Robertson; Ian Gray
Front row: Sheena Swanson; Audrey Harcus; Elizabeth Cromarty; Mamie Hay; Marnie Bertram; Florrie Tait

opened again on that site. It was a huge gap in our lives for a time. Dougie, however, got things up and running again a few months later in the then unused 'Naval cinema', which served until the Phoenix opened in 1955.

Variety concerts were also popular, and some of us spent a whole winter involved in one, organised by Mrs Tait of Quoyburray, along with some helpers. We performed in a variety of places; Kirkwall, Deerness, Holm and Tankerness, amongst others. The chorus girls were Audrey Harcus, Maimie Hay, Elizabeth Cromarty and Marnie Bertram; duets and solos were sung by Sheena Swanson and John Flett; sketches and club swinging were performed by Ian Gray, Jim Robertson and myself, and Highland dancing was by Florrie Tait. The highlight of the show was probably *The Toorie on his Bonnet*, sung by Louis Macdonald complete with kilt and *toorie*. Most of the concerts finished with a dance in the local hall.

Dancing was always popular, and, apart from the BB Club, the Scout Club, school dances, the Saturday night 'hop' at the Cosmo, or the occasional wedding, there were the various 'society balls' in Kirkwall. No chance of us getting a ticket for them, but there were sometimes openings for a cloakroom job, or working behind the lemonade counter. They were usually held in the 'Cosmo Ballroom', later 'Casablanca' and now a car showroom. No alcohol was sold on the premises, not that there was any shortage, but soft drinks were provided and that is where we came in. I had a great contact in WHB Sutherland, my boss at the time, who got me in as cloakroom or lemonade boy on many occasions. There were some *crabby* old 'so-and-so's' who gave us loads of abuse for 'crushing' their best overcoats. It was difficult to do anything else with each pigeonhole measuring about nine inches square. The pay was not brilliant but there were lots of good 'tippers' around, and the entertainment gained from watching Kirkwall's 'elite' letting their hair down was almost reward enough.

Play was important and the amount of freedom we had in an area of no small risk engendered elements of trust and responsibility. We learned how to look after ourselves. We also learned about nature: how to handle the various fish and shellfish we found; how to recognise birds, their eggs and other wildlife; what to pick up and what to leave well alone - especially during the war; how to climb cliffs and rocks safely; how to handle boats; something about tides and the dangers they presented, and we learned how to swim - essential when you are surrounded by water. We took risks as all kids do, but they were mostly calculated and we rarely came to any real harm. We were never bored, and even though the facilities available were limited, we adjusted what there was to suit our purposes. The whole town and the surrounding area was our playground and 'leisure centre'. There was always plenty to do, indoors or out, some of it organised but mostly spontaneous, and a lot of it included the whole family. Having said that, playing by yourself was never a problem. There was always a jigsaw.

Message boys . . .

Message boys were in demand in the 1940s, which offered an opportunity for us to make a bit of pocket money. The pay was not brilliant; ten shillings (50p) for after school hours and all day Saturday, amounting to fourteen hours a week. During the holidays, for a full week of forty-four hours, over five-and-a-half days, it rose to £1. Delivery vans have now done away with our services almost totally, I suspect.

Some shops had their own proper message bikes, with a cage attachment in front of the handlebars which held a large shop basket. They were not the easiest things to ride, as the cage did not move when you turned the handlebars, and this could be a bit disconcerting. I used my own bike, and the basket had to be balanced precariously on the handlebars with one hand while you steered with the other. It sounds great fun, but cycling up hills, in rain, wind or snow, or sometimes all three, with a sizeable load of breakables in the basket, had its drawbacks.

Pleasures of being a message boy

I started at WHB Sutherland's chemist shop in 1946, and my time there was an experience I thoroughly enjoyed. Everyone there was very helpful at a time in any boy's life that holds its fair share of 'growing pains'; which was, in my case, a particularly difficult time. Bill Sutherland - I don't think I ever called him that, but I thought of him as Bill - took over the mantle of 'father figure' in 1947, after my father died suddenly. For that I will always remember him with the greatest affection.

God knows I tried his patience to the full with a series of unfortunate mishaps. He said nothing when I broke the back window while kicking a ball about in the backyard. He still said nothing when I dropped his total monthly allocation of olive oil, a full winchester, on to a concrete floor where it unfortunately broke. He made no accusations when I decided to repair a loose toilet seat with a hammer and a screwdriver, and the back of the toilet fell off. It almost got to him, however, when I tried to cure a dripping pipe in the store behind 80, Victoria Street, which he rented from the Royal Hotel. The problem was that the old lead sink, where the drip was falling, held all the big winchesters and other containers that were waiting to be sent back to the manufacturers for re-use. The labels were becoming unstuck which made things difficult, and I decided that with the blunt edge of an axe under the rolled-over lead pipe, from which the tap had been removed, I would be able to stop the drip with a few taps of a hammer. It wasn't a bad theory but it didn't work, and, to cut a long story short, by the time the plumber arrived most of the floor was submerged under four inches of water. This was where the bales of cotton wool, lint and other absorbent materials were kept. I can't remember exactly what he said, but I made a conscious decision then to leave repairs alone. I continued to work happily there, however, until I left school in 1949 and began an apprenticeship as a joiner.

Best laid schemes . . .

The duties of a message boy, wherever you worked, were wide and varied, even without repairing anything. You were basically a 'gopher', at the beck and call of everyone who worked there, but there were certain regular duties that you became familiar with. At Sutherland's, the first job on arrival at 4.30pm, after school, was to deliver any medicines to individual homes, and on Mondays there were also the Balfour Hospital supplies. After that, a sinkful of measures, mortars, pestles, bottles, and all the other things concerned with dispensing medicines, had to be washed. For obvious reasons this was something that had to be done meticulously, and, apart from soap powder, there were two acids available in bottles that were used for difficult items. Rinsing them after use was very important, and a strict routine had to be followed. Poisons were always kept in dark green, ribbed bottles.

Personal shopping came into it, and every Saturday morning there was a visit to Leith's, the butchers, for a pound of 'special sausages' and a pound of liver for Bill's cat. That was the message, and I never discovered whether or not the sausages were for the cat as well. Perhaps if I had asked for them in a different way I may have found out.

Stocking shelves took a fair bit of time. Most of the immediate stock was either in the back store or up in the attic above the main shop. There was also storage space rented in what was the old Post Office (where the Victoria Hairdressing Salon is now), also in part of the back store at William Shearer's, and of course in the ill-fated store behind 80, Victoria Street. Sprinkling the shop floor with water to keep the dust down was always done before sweeping; windows had to be washed regularly, especially during the school holidays, and I was even entrusted to do the big ones at the front of the shop.

You soon became an expert in all things medical - not that I tried to put this into practice, I hasten to add. Occasionally, however, under supervision, I was allowed to weigh out 'powders' for medical purposes, count out tablets and fill up bottles with medicine from a larger container.

One 'job' I always enjoyed, about 5pm every Saturday, was to go down to Wattie Lobban's on Broad Street, or preferably into the Cosy Café, where I had a coffee. My remit was to note down the football results from the radio so that Bill could check his pools. It usually took till about 6 o'clock, finishing time, and it made a grand end to the working week.

Bill was a keen sportsman, daft on football, and many an hour he spent telling me about the great players who played for Celtic or Kirkwall Rovers when he was young. He never missed a Rovers match, senior or junior, and went to many other matches as well. He played golf whenever he had time, and tennis and badminton, well into middle age. He was also held in great respect among the business community of the town. As far as I can remember he never owned a car, but cycled everywhere.

I grew seven inches in the three years I worked there, mainly thanks again to Bill's generosity. Every day, at 5pm, he had his tea at the sink in the back shop. This was because he had books to do after the shop closed at six o'clock, and maybe a football match to go to before going home. I put on the kettle, made the tea and waited patiently, standing about one yard away from where he sat until he could ignore me no longer. With exasperation written all over his face he would hand me half of his 'piece', and only then could he settle down to reading his paper and eating what was left of his tea. I was a growing boy.

During the holidays there was barely enough to keep an enterprising and industrious young lad going, not even one like me, so I spent many hours up in the old store chopping firewood, often in the company of old Jimmy Bews, who worked at William Shearer's shop across the street. He had a glass eye, which he used to take out and show me, warning me that it was the result of an accident incurred while chopping firewood. Once a year, I was delegated to build the winter's supply of peats in the garage up at Ardmhor, where the Sutherlands lived. The lorry load was tipped in the driveway and it took a whole day to cart them inside and build them into a peatstack.

Stocktaking was a busy time. Everyone was involved. Every shelf, cupboard, drawer, and all the stores had to be checked and totalled. It took days.

The shop itself was vastly different to what it is now. It had a front shop, about one third the current size; a back shop or dispensary with the small office off; a store behind which held the small toilet with the loose seat, and the supply of olive oil, and the aforementioned attic store above. It was not the easiest area to work in as the sloping eaves meant that you were bent double all the time you were up there. Shelving had been installed in every available space and everything was kept in strict order. The back shop was not big, but it was where the dispensing, washing up, eating, making up parcels, and everything that was done, got done. It could become quite congested at times. Heating was supplied in this area by a paraffin stove.

The front shop was packed with all sorts of patent medicines, mostly displayed in oak wall cabinets with glass doors, or stored lower down in shelved wall units with wooden flaps that pulled down. Every conceivable space was used. There was a top shelf that ran round three walls containing large coloured bottles of chemicals. The shelf that always caught my attention was the one that stored the large bottle of barley sugar sweeties. There was also a drawer in the back shop, which held the various cough sweeties, such as Horlicks tablets, blackcurrant pastilles and Zubes. Next to barley sugar, Horlicks tablets were my favourite. There was a counter on one side of the front shop, and a glass display cabinet on the other, with a high unit between which kept the public from seeing through into the back shop.

It was a happy place to work; the people there were great to work with, or perhaps work under would be more accurate. There were the two chemists, John Mainland and Alistair Doloughan; the dispenser, Ian Flett; Ella Flett, a really gentle soul, and, of course, Bill's daughter, Janet.

The experience of being a message boy was good, and it is a pity in some ways that it is a job that is no longer available to young lads. It introduces you gently to the idea of earning a living, working with people and using your initiative, even if it is not always appreciated. All in all, I enjoyed it and it was with some regret that I left to move into the 'man's' world. I did a lot of growing up there, in every sense.

'Big bites o'fish
and peedie bites o'tattie' . . .

This was advice given to my grandmother-in-law when fish was plentiful but would not keep, and *tatties* had to last over the winter. It illustrates how diet varied with the seasons according to what was readily available at any particular time.

There were no fridges or freezers; food was preserved by pickling it with salt, or by drying. When our grandparents were children, I guess they did not always have enough to eat, certainly not enough of the things they needed for a balanced diet, yet most of them survived, many to a ripe old age. I cannot say that I was ever hungry, but that was mainly due to my mum, who, like most mothers of her generation, was an excellent manager, cook and baker, and clearly understood the principles of nutrition. Having said that, I accept that parents with large families did struggle to keep everyone happy, and it was often a case of 'De'il tak' the hindmost'. There was one occasion when a father was carving a cocky chicken to share amongst his several children, and the requests began pouring in: 'I want a leg, Dadda,' from at least five of the ravenous brood. In exasperation he announced, 'This is a chicken I'm carving, no' a b——y spider.' How it was eventually rationed out goodness knows, but he did have a point.

Probably about three-quarters of what we ate was produced at home, or acquired more or less free. Some meat and fish were bought, mostly the cheaper cuts such as pork knees or stew, but tripe was not a thing eaten very often in our house. Morning rolls and bread, baked by Flett and Sons, Gardens, or Groundwaters, and later CT Stewarts; biscuits, particularly *coorse* biscuits, and occasionally a '*Youma*' loaf as a treat, were purchased, but little else in the way of bread, and virtually no cakes. We used to go for new rolls for breakfast before going to school. The range of biscuits available now epitomises the huge choice of foodstuffs in shops today. In our young days, biscuits came in large tins, not in packets, and they were weighed out as required. The broken ones left in the bottom could be had at half price in most shops. They tasted just as good, maybe even better. The only sweet biscuits I can remember are rich tea, digestive, ginger snaps, ones with cream or jam in the middle, and digestives with dark chocolate on one side as a special. There may have been others, but not many. The arrival of the Penguin and the mint Yoyo heralded an explosion in the biscuit world that we would not have believed possible. This could equally be said about sweets, fruit, canned foods, drinks - soft and alcoholic - and many other things.

Oatcakes, bere bannocks, flour bannocks, big pancakes, scones of all kinds - drop, fruit, treacle, wheat, *sooans*, oven, girdle, *tatty*, fatty (lovely with syrup) - gingerbread, shortbread, buns, rock buns, sponges, fly cemeteries, melting moments, doodle bugs, kisses and many other delicacies, were all baked at home. The smell of baking always whetted the appetite, and many a scone and butter was eaten before it had a chance to cool. Most houses had access to a 'plot', where *tatties,* garden *neeps,* cabbage, lettuce, carrots, onions, leeks, beetroot, peas, radishes, parsley, cress, cauliflower and other vegetables, were grown.

Butter, eggs, including duck eggs, cheese, an occasional hen or cocky chicken, a rabbit, a hare, a wild duck, or other 'country fare', were sent in from Shapinsay on a regular basis. I think some money did change hands for this, but not at shop prices. All this was supplemented by *partans*, lobsters, *sillocks, cuithes, pootties* and other fish; *spoots*, cockles, whelks and other *ebb meat*; wild birds' eggs, such as *teeicks* or *dunters*, etc. A special treat was a dried *sillock*, or *cuithe*, baked outside in the sun for days until hard and chewy, which was then skinned and eaten like a bar of toffee. *Home brew*, ginger wine and other wines made from *tatties* or rhubarb, were produced for the festive season.

Normally we ate at the table, and good manners were encouraged, often by a rap over the knuckles with a knife or fork. Breakfast was mostly cereal, wheat flakes or bran, often with hot milk in cold weather, new rolls, or toast to use up older bread, scrambled or boiled eggs, and a glass of milk, again hot with sugar on cold days.

Dinners were always in the middle of the day, and usually consisted of two courses; soup and meat, or meat and *pud*. Home-made soups were normally made with a bone, preferably a marrow bone, from which we spooned out the remaining marrow afterwards. They included lentil, pea, vegetable, *tatty*, Scotch broth, chicken, and, on one memorable occasion, fish. We rebelled against it and it was never offered again. Soup was usually accompanied by *bere* bannocks or oatcakes, either buttered or broken up and mixed in.

Main courses were wide and varied; fish at least once a week, meat on some days and things made from left-overs when necessary in the form of patties, stovies, etc. A cocky chicken with gravy made from the giblets, along with new *tatties,* was a real treat. There was also the wide range of game and *ebb meat* to add variety. Boiled or mashed *tatties*, or *clapshot*, were dished up with most meals, and if there was any left over it was fried the next day. *Tatties* were a big thing, and the preference for various varieties such as Long blues, Kerr's pinks, Keppleton Kidneys etc, was very strong. Not so popular with kids, but deemed necessary, were boiled fish, salt fish and salt herring, but the *tatties* and dripping that went with them were good. On holiday once I excused myself from staying for dinner at Elwick, as I knew that salt herring was on the menu, tramped the good mile to Brecks in time for dinner, only to find that it was salt herring there as well. This was bound to happen, as a supply had just arrived at the various shops on that particular day and practically every house on the island was having salt herring. Oysters or clams we never saw as children, even though they are available in Orkney waters, and we didn't eat mussels.

Puddings seemed to be mostly of the milky variety; custard, cremola, sago, semolina, tapioca, junket, rice, curds and whey, and if there was a tin of fruit to go with it, that was something special. Even prunes were a fine change. Strawberries and cream, at certain times of year, were wonderful. The war affected us very little food-wise, apart from the rationing of baking ingredients, as most of what we ate before 1939 was still available.

Tea was not normally a cooked meal, but a huge spread of home bakes of all sorts, farm cheese and butter, home-made jam, curd or marmalade, and a glass of milk or tea. Coffee was not often drunk, and when we did have it, it was usually made from 'Camp' coffee out of a bottle. Syrup, which tended to blacken tea, was used as a sugar substitute when it was in short supply.

Supper was, more often than not, *coorse* biscuits and butter, or toast, along with a glass of

Toast for supper

milk. That is, if we had not found the where-with-all for a *patty supper* on the way home. Toast was made sitting in front of the fire, with bread, a scone, a pancake, or anything else we fancied, stuck on a fork, and held as close to the glowing embers as was comfortable. Yellow flames were no good, they only blackened the bread with smoke. Bread got *feesked* after a few days, but if we gave it a wee scrape to get the green bits off, it toasted lovely. Farm butter tended to go off after a time, and though we ate it, *rancid* butter was not that great. Milk, too, got sour in hot weather, but even if it curdled in tea it was not too bad to drink provided it was not too far gone. It was not as good as *kirn* milk, the milk remaining after making butter, which was always on hand for baking. It had a lovely sharp taste.

Nothing was wasted. I remember old Mrs Foubister, who lived next door, telling us that she always skinned the *neb* and feet of a hen to make stock for soup. She also used the feathers for pillows.

Eating out was never thought of, apart from a visit to the chip shop, to Zanre's café, or 'Peedie Charlie's. Donnie Chalmers' patties were, and still are, unequalled, and his fish or sausage suppers were not bad either. They were always served in a *poke*, and if they were to be taken home they were wrapped in an old newspaper. The queues outside his shop were very long after the *pictures* came out, or after a football match, but it was always worth the wait. Scott's fish shop in Bridge Street also sold fish and chips, but not on a regular basis.

Another unparalleled product was Zanre's ice cream. Mr and Mrs Zanre were Italian and their range of milk shakes, strawberry ices, hot orange or lemon, coffee etc, was excellent, and when pocket money allowed their 'Central Café' was a favourite haunt. It continued under temporary management during the war, when Mr Zanre suffered the indignity of being interned. 'Peedie Charlie's' was another popular spot, run by a very likeable guy, and though Charlie Celli was also of Italian descent, he was, I believe, born in Inverness. He told us once he had never been to Italy in his life and had no ambition to go. He was the only person I can remember who could retain the ash of a whole cigarette, adhered to the stump and held in his mouth until it was done. He never put it down - he was too busy - and he was seldom without one.

School treats were purchased from Louie Foubister at the Rocky Shop at the head of the Strynd, or from Brass's shop, situated diagonally across the road before it was pulled down. When we 'discovered' the Nicholson family's bake shop down the lane at the Big Tree, where they produced the most scrumptious meringues, cream cookies and sugary cookies ever made, it became the popular haunt for break time treats. The queues at playtime and lunchtime were long and, with only fifteen minutes to work on at playtime, the race down the Strynd and up again was more like a stampede. If you weren't there early you were too late.

'Sweeties', rationed for about six years by the war, and all the other years by a lack of spending money, were available at lots of shops around *the toon*. Our local sweetie shops were Bella Gray's, Cutt's and Grant's, all in the St Catherine's Place area. Black pipes, straps and laces, red and black, all made of liquorice; a lucky bag, when you were flush, gob stoppers, bulls' eyes, barley sugar sticks, pan drops, the occasional bar of Highland toffee, liquorice allsorts, striped balls, sherbet dabs, with a black liquorice tube to suck it with; 'tube tubes', chocolate beans, caramels, lollipops and many others; they were all there. Toffee lasted longer and this made it very popular. Bulls' eyes and gobstoppers were brilliant, lasting for ages, especially if they had been in the pocket several times, as it took a lot of sucking to get through the coating of fluff. Apart from bars of toffee or chocolate or 'lucky bags', sweeties did not come in packets or wrappers. Everything was on display in large jars and what you asked for had to be weighed out carefully. There was always one held back in the shopkeeper's fingers which was either dropped in at the last minute to give good measure or, much to the dismay of the purchaser, popped back into the jar again. Half the fun was in the picking and choosing, and it says a lot for the patience of the shopkeepers that they were prepared to take so much time with us, for all we had to spend.

One treat, which we got on a Monday when a certain relative was visiting from Shapinsay, was an acid drop which had been in his pocket for a day or two. His contribution to our sweetie ration was 'a quarter o' drapth', which he carried with him until they were done. At home we made toffee.

Outside we devoured all sorts of titbits. We ate heather berries, sucked honey out of clover, *curly dodies* and fuchsia, pinched field *neeps*, sucked wild mint and *sooricks*, chewed seaweed, grasses and oats of various kinds, ate 'cheese' extracted from thistles, wild peas found in small black pods, etc. Much of it was very tasty, although I suspect that very little of it would appeal to children now.

Our diet was governed by what was available and what we could afford, but it was well balanced and we seemed to thrive on it well enough.

Home cures and doctors . . .

With such a healthy lifestyle you would think that we would have had no problems, and for most of us that was true, apart from the usual measles, mumps, chickenpox, etc. Colds and other 'minor ailments' were not things that you stayed at home for and classes were frequently full of coughing, sneezing kids. Things were passed on in this way, and normally you went as long as you could crawl. It helped to build up a sort of resistance. Preventative medicine was the big thing. We were regularly confronted by a variety of vitamin tablets and tonics, particularly in winter. Iron tablets, Metatone (an iron-based tonic), cod liver oil by the spoonful, Haliborange capsules, Virol, extract of malt, often combined with cod liver oil, Andrews liver salts, Epsom salts, and so on. All this was intended to stop us from getting colds, 'flu, or worse, and clearly it seemed to work quite well as much of it is still on the market.

As doctors had to be paid two shillings and sixpence per visit, it was essential to be sure that he or she (in our case it was always a he) was necessary before making use of his services. Things changed in 1948 with the introduction of the National Health Service, and we were suddenly free to go without having to consider the cost. Doctors, like teachers and ministers, were held in high esteem, and considered to be 'pillars of society'. They also tended to be fairly static. Unless you had the service of a '*howdie*', the doctor who brought you into the world was usually with you all through childhood and beyond. The value of this was that he knew all about you and you knew him. He was very much the family doctor. They did not have the opt-out of a 'virus', or the support of a wide range of antibiotics, so they had to come up with a name for whatever was 'gan aboot' and provide a cure, which they frequently did. Our family's health was initially in the hands of Dr Sinclair, until just after the war, when he was replaced by Dr Gordon.

There were two surgeries Monday to Saturday, one early afternoon and the other early evening. There were no appointments, and consultations were on a 'first-come first-served' basis unless there were children waiting, as they got priority. Everybody who came was seen by the doctor. House calls, when necessary, were part of the service. When Moyra, as a child, was threatening pneumonia, Dr Emslie called daily and used to sit on the bed and chat for a while and even play games.

There were three practices in Kirkwall, each with a single doctor and a receptionist, to cater for the whole town and much of the surrounding area. Medicines were often prescribed and made up on the premises. The big fears were tuberculosis, diphtheria, meningitis, polio and scarlet fever, and with no cures available at that time patients were isolated in special wards at Eastbank Hospital. Several school friends died from one of these dreaded diseases. The Balfour Hospital, with one resident surgeon, Mr Mclure, handled the rest. When visiting someone in hospital it was a regular practice to go for a bottle of 'clean' water from the spring at the Peedie Sea, or from the one at the Willows, to take up with you.

TB, or consumption, was only too common, and though it was often fatal, many only becoming aware that they had had it when it showed up at a later date on an x-ray. Inoculations were a major new break through, administered under the eagle eye of Dr Bannerman, the Medical Officer of Health. The first one we had was for diphtheria, and we got it along with the nurses at Eastbank, as our parents were, at the time, helping out with the caretaking duties of the hospital.

We avoided doctors as much as possible. Apart from being treated for the usual childhood illnesses, medication was administered at home. One problem, however, which bothered a lot of the boys at this time, self-inflicted to a degree, manifested itself in persistent ear infections and stys. This was due to regular swimming in the 'Basin' amongst oil, sewage, and other equally unpleasant things. Many a 'wigging-off' we got from Doc Gordon, who knew exactly what the cause was.

Home remedies were wide-ranging and had mixed success. Many were passed down through the generations, and some of the more successful ones are still in use. Dettol was the big 'cleaner' for all bumps, cuts and bruises. Bumps on the head which raised a lump were smeared with a 'nob' of butter. All cuts and bruises were treated with Germoline or iodine, and usually bandaged with a strip of cotton torn from an old pillowcase or other suitable item. *Plooks* and blackheads were squeezed to remove the infection. Boils and other more serious infections were covered with a poultice, made from bread, soaked in water, as hot as you could bear, then wrapped in a piece of cloth. It was replaced as often as necessary until the problem 'came to a head', burst, and the infection drained. An alternative was a black treacly substance, bought from the chemist, which also drew out any infection. Nettle stings were treated with the slimy bit of a 'dockan', while other stings or bites were usually 'cured' with iodine. 'Picked' knees, or cracked lips, were smeared with Vaseline, Glymel jelly, or Snowfire. Eye infections were bathed in warm water and salt, or soothed with Golden Eye Ointment. Football knocks got better much faster after rubbing in veterinary embrocation, or 'horse liniment', which was much stronger than Sloan's. Toothache was treated by chewing a clove, or by covering the problem tooth with cotton wool, soaked in oil of cloves, or, better still, whisky.

Sore stomachs initiated a glass of boiled water or milk, a dose of milk of magnesia, or, if all else failed, a drop of brandy in water. Constipation called for drastic measures. Sumptuous helpings of prunes, senna pods, spoonfuls of syrup of figs, Cascara, or liquid paraffin, were liberally administered, and everyone avoided you like a ticking time bomb, until you became 'regular' again. 'Hot spots' brought out the black treacle and sulphur, along with the application of baking soda paste, Calamine Lotion or talcum powder, to cool them down. Coughs, colds and sore throats were 'sweated' out with hot drinks and hot water bottles, a sweaty sock tied round the throat, and inhaling steam under a towel. Thermogene pads were strapped to the chest, after rubbing in Vick, and if you were in luck you got a stiff 'toddy' made from whisky, sugar and hot water. This was backed up with cough sweeties, such as Zubes or blackcurrant pastilles, and by gargling with salt and water. Salt and water was also used as a mouthwash for ulcers. Aspirin was the only headache cure. Warts were removed by tying a piece of thread tightly round them, to cut off the blood supply, until they dried up and fell off. Impetigo, quite common, was painted with Gentian Violet, a bright purple substance that stained clothes badly and was there for all to see. Scabies was attacked by fastidiously washing the body and clothes. Potential blisters and chilblains were eased with surgical or methylated spirits. Anyone who was 'chesty' had to be kept in as much as possible in cold weather, protected by plenty of warm, dry clothes, fed with a nourishing broth and dosed with a tonic to try and improve the appetite. Recovery was usually slow.

Home medication – the full treatment

At the other extreme, outbreaks of head lice were attacked with paraffin, Derbac soap and a fine-toothed comb. After washing the hair severely, paraffin was liberally applied, and you knelt with your head over a newspaper. If anything fell out during the combing process, you squeezed it with great delight. Fleas were sought by undressing in a bath of water, in the belief that the unwelcome guest would leap into the water, but in all honesty I never ever saw one do this. This was followed by a frantic search among clothes and bedclothes, and a scream of delight if successful, or a groan of disgust if you missed it. DDT powder was used successfully for many years, until it was considered to be a health hazard - for the person as well as the flea.

Doctors' remedies, though more scientific, were often much worse to take: bottles of foul-tasting medicines or powders, washed down with lemonade; something that nearly put you off lemonade for life. Health was in some ways more precarious, but having to overcome more illnesses without much help probably made us more resilient. It is surprising how many of the 'old-fashioned' home cures are still in use; as they had no scientific basis, their origins must have been founded more on intuition. Whatever it was it helped, and all things considered we were just as healthy as kids are now.

Mostly 'claes' . . .

The title 'Fashion' would hardly fit this section, though there were definite trends that influenced what we wore. Practical considerations such as cost, wear and warmth had much more to do with it, particularly when our parents had the major say.

Quantity was controlled during the war by the availability of coupons, but in most cases financial restraints were already in place. There were clear divides. We had clothes for 'Sunday best'; suits and best shoes for boys, usually with a white shirt and sometimes a tie; frocks, coats and hats, sometimes to match, for girls. Moyra, when she was a girl, was given a new dress and coat to match from her Gran every year. School clothes were hard-wearing, warm and roomy, but reasonably dressy. Finally, there were play clothes, usually older school clothes, supplemented by dungarees, *plimmies*, if you had them, and rubber boots for wet or snowy weather.

'Hand-me-downs' were a big thing, and having several older cousins was considered to be a great asset - by the parents, that is. They were not so popular with the child who was lumbered with something that did not fit, and obviously did not look like much, otherwise it would have been worn out before you got it. Alterations, particularly to the length of leg in long trousers, were almost always needed. The first pair of *longs* that I wore were 'inherited' and I hated them - baggy round the behind, and *nippit* about the ankles, something that would have been perfect during some of the more recent trends, but not then, and certainly not for me. They got pretty rough treatment, and thankfully did not last very long. Some donations were re-made; big *breeks* were made into small *breeks*, often without pockets. There was nothing to put in them anyhow.

Trousers were held up by *straps,* fashionable among the jet set now, but we were far happier when belts came along. During the war, the acquisition of a 'Navy' belt was a bit special. It was about three inches wide, made of dark blue canvas and leather, with a double buckle and a leather pocket to keep things in. There were a lot of years to get through, however, before *longs* were a problem. Boys rarely got into long *breeks* before going into the 'big' school, and some continued in short trousers into their early teens. They were mostly big guys, which was just as well or they would have come in for a fair bit of ribbing. Short *breeks*, 'scratchy' flannel shirts and home-knitted *gansys* were the order of the day, along with home-knitted knee-length socks held up by garters made of broad, black elastic. Footwear consisted of heavy leather shoes, or preferably boots if you had some distance to cover to get to school. Boots usually had leather laces, and the life of the soles was extended by applying metal toe and heel caps, with *protectors* inserted over the remaining area. Kicking up sparks on the pavement was another use for them. Underwear was limited, with two, or at the very most, three, changes at differing stages of wear being the 'norm'. We also had 'warm' stuff for winter, usually with longer legs and arms and made from thicker, itchier, material. We did not, could not, change every day as clothes' washing was only done once a week, but then we did not have a shower every morning either, basically because we did not have a shower. Pyjamas were not all that common, so vest and drawers usually had to double up for them as well. In all honesty, I suppose, we weren't as sweet smelling as kids are today, but, as we were all in the same boat, it was not a problem. We all smelt the same.

Two items that, after much protest, I was eventually excused from wearing, were 'combinations' and helmets. 'Combinations', some home-knitted, were a kind of undergarment, invented by a sadist, which covered you from just above the elbow, up to the neck, then all the way down to just above the knee, and all in a 'oner'. There was a necessary divide, low down, front and back, but apart from that you were enshrined, almost suffocated, in this contraption, mortified at the thought of anyone discovering that you were wearing such a thing. They were meant to prevent you getting colds in winter. Most of us would sooner have had pneumonia.

Some winter comforts

Helmets, made of leather, were another winter garment, shaped like a sort of skull cap, that only allowed your face, from just above the eyes to peep out under the brim. They were strapped on firmly under the chin, and had earflaps that could be opened or shut with a metal fastener, depending on whether or not you wanted to hear.

Patches, usually of leather or rexine, were used to repair elbows on jumpers or jackets, and knees on *longs*. They were usually neatly sewn on, but the invention of Copydex later on made the application simpler, even if it meant not being able to bend an elbow or knee for a day or two.

The helmet

There was also the question of 'growing-room'. Everything that fitted beautifully, clothing or footwear, was discarded in favour of at least a size bigger to allow for 'growing room'. By the time it fitted it was done and ready for the bin. Hands and feet vanished under a new suit, and shoes that allowed lots of space for growth inevitably blistered heels.

We were *coorse* on shoes, particularly Sunday shoes, as they were by far the best for kicking stones and tins and anything else that needed kicking. Sandals were not popular with boys - too 'cissyish'. Another common type of footwear was 'feeticks', a sort of knitted slipper that was worn inside during the winter. They did not look like much, but they were very comfortable and kept the feet lovely and warm

In spite of our difficulties, however, we did have 'trendy' ideas from time to time. Dungarees were considered to be very 'cool', though that particular meaning of the word was not yet in vogue. Dungarees with a 'rule' pocket, even if you did not have a 'rule', were really good, and dungarees with 'rule' and 'bib' pockets were very 'grown-up'. They wore out, but of course the modern idea of wearing them riddled with holes was not for us. We would have been ashamed to go out with torn clothing, or at least our parents would have been ashamed for us. Holes had to be patched, agreed unanimously by parents and children. Anything else was 'scruffy'. Dungaree *breeks* came in later, long before jeans were invented.

New suit

Home-knitted *jerseys* were also brilliant. Older garments which were getting past repair were often unravelled, the wool rolled into balls for knitting into new jumpers, socks, balaclavas, or whatever. Like most mums of the time, mine was a great knitter, mainly by necessity, but she enjoyed doing it long after the need was gone. Polo necks, navy, grey, or better still, white, were always welcome, especially if knitted with a 'cable' pattern. Kitted out in a white cable roll neck, a pair of dungaree trousers, and a pair of thigh length, white, sea-boot stockings, rolled down over the tops of the rubber boots, fisherman style, and you really felt a million dollars. Add to that a navy blue Norwegian *toorie*, with a white band round the edge, a 'pom-pom' on top and you were made.

Balaclavas had a mixed reception. Popular during the war, in winter, they could be worn with only your eyes in sight above the shoulders, or rolled up to sit on top of the head like a sort of bonnet. Later ones had brims and were much trendier. Berets were worn by some, but not with any enthusiasm, and caps were even less popular. There was a short-lived phase, during our early teens, when we tried to acquire felt hats. Mine was bought at Archie Kemp's for £1, and to this day I grudge every penny of it. It was a heck of a lot of money at the time, and the hat was only worn about three times before the whole idea fell flat.

Fair Isle jumpers suddenly became the 'in' thing, and I remember my mother knitting me a beauty, with navy background and covered with a lovely pattern in all sorts of bright colours. It had a zip in the polo neck so that you could have it open with a tie. I wore it under my jacket to the BB Club for the first time, with only one sleeve. I just couldn't wait for it to be finished.

Moving into early teens, Harris tweed jackets and flannels were the smart things to be seen in. Hepworths was the place to go, and Jack Clark always kept us up to scratch with the latest styles and colours, made to measure if you could afford it. Short socks were worn under the flannels, and I remember feeling particularly grown up when a neighbouring gentleman presented me with a pair of 'suspenders' to keep my socks up. 'Spivvy' ties became the 'in' thing;

the gaudier, fancier and more colourful the better. Tie pins became a bit of rage, and if you had one with a small chain to loop the tie through, that was real style. Miniature military badges on tiepins for boys or as brooches for girls were very 'with it'.

Late in the war, and after it, the jerkin, a bit like a tunic, gave way to army or RAF 'battledress' tops. Better still if you acquired a pilot's flying jacket, fleecy-lined and made of leather. They were really special and were worn summer and winter even if you were roasting inside. All in all, by the time we were teenagers, it was little wonder that we were ready to experiment with new ideas, heard about from the *Sooth*. 'Drain-pipes', bootlace ties, 'winkle-pickers', 'brothel-creepers' and so on, soon began to be worn by the teenage lads in Kirkwall.

There were other things that affected your appearance that were important. Haircuts for instance, were mostly done at home with a pair of scissors, and tidied up with a pair of hand clippers if you had them. Styles did not exist. The nearest modern example would be a 'No 1', or maybe more like a 'No 2', but slightly longer, often with a tuft left at the front. I suppose there were practical reasons for this with head lice being a fairly common thing. Girls had problems too, with pigtails being about the only alternative to shoulder-length hair. The war changed things quite a bit, and 'the sleek' was the thing to have.

Hair, a lot longer, was plastered flat over the head with generous applications of 'Brylcream' or 'Brilliantine'. Brilliantine was very much like 3-in-1 oil with a bit of perfume, and did wonders for the pillow at night. 'Nufix' was cleaner but acted more like cement, and your hair went rock hard after using it. Jocky Sinclair was the man to go to if you wanted to come out with a 'proper sleek' on. Words like 'dabber', 'swank' and 'spiv' suddenly became important, and we began to look for improvements in our appearance. That was about it, however, until the DA (apparently named after a 'duck's arse' because of the resemblance) came along, but that was much later.

Changing 'fashions' – then and now

The need to shave arrived, but few of us took a chance with the 'cut-throat' razor. The safety razor with a 'Blue Gillette' blade was the favourite, and small bits of newspaper or toilet roll were stuck on any cuts until they stopped bleeding. After Christmas you may have had a bottle of 'Old Spice' aftershave to soothe the face with, and make you smell nice - the adjective 'sexy' had not yet arrived for aftershave.

One item, vaguely connected with appearance, is a watch. They were few and far between. Watches did not seem so important then, yet much of our daily routine depended on knowing the time. We seemed to develop a fairly accurate inner clock, which was aided by the regular chimes of the Cathedral if you lived in Kirkwall.

The subject of women's fashions at this time is something better left to them to describe, but there were certain noticeable changes. Sailors' bell-bottom trousers became very popular and undoubtedly led to the start of women regularly wearing trousers - how we have lived to regret that particular trend. Parachute silk, acquired from service personnel, was popular for making underclothes apparently, and things like 'pixies' became fashionable for a time. From what my wife tells me, I think it is fair to say that they were as glad to see the back of the 'liberty bodice', navy knickers and home-knitted stockings held up by garters, as boys were to get rid of short *breeks*, hairy *simmets*, long socks and garters. As they say, if you don't have the legs for it, don't wear it. At least we were not subjected to the kilt. *Claes* are certainly different now.

Balfour Village area – showing Gatehouse, Balfour Castle and 'Plantings'.
Elwick farm and mill in foreground

Holidays . . .

Holidays were as popular in the 1930s and '40s as they are now, but going out of Orkney was rare and going abroad hardly ever heard of. When the BBs went to camp in Aberdeen in 1948 most of the group had never been *Sooth*.

Almost without exception all my holidays were spent in Shapinsay with various relatives, and what fabulous holidays they were. During the war permits were required to move between the islands, but since both my parents came from Shapinsay we seemed to have been exempt, and as parents did not have much in the way of holidays then, my sister and I usually went to Shapinsay on our own. There seemed to be even more scope for games and adventure in the country, particularly on a farm, than in Kirkwall, and that was saying something.

The voyage out through the bay, across 'The String' and into Shapinsay pier took about half an hour, which was long enough if the sea was up. Normally we went on the old *Iona*, a wooden boat built in Shapinsay and their answer to the *Vital Spark*. It had two cabins, one fore and one aft, for the comfort of the passengers. On privileged occasions I would get down into the engine room to watch Robbie Groat tending his engines with loving care. When the *Iona* was not available a smaller motor boat, the *Klydon*, made the trip, and if all else failed Willie Nicolson's *Sheena* crossed between Carness and Shapinsay. All in all, Shapinsay had a great boat service mainly thanks to the Dennison family. Transport from the pier was on foot if you were not too far away from your destination, but a horse and cart or a pony and gig usually came for us if we were going farther up the island.

Days spent in the village area were usually with my aunt at the gardener's cottage in the grounds of Balfour Castle. As it wasn't far we walked, but only via prescribed routes following a path up past the back of the gatehouse, across the main drive and in through a small track amongst the trees to the house. The alternative was the 'long' trek to the far end of the village and up the 'tradesmen's entrance' towards Sound. On no account did we walk up the main drive. This was serious stuff - if we trespassed into *the plantings* or garden areas to play or pinch berries and were caught, we were in big trouble. Many a rollicking we got from my uncle-in-law, John Liddell, the head gardener, or his dad, old Willie Liddell, whose *bawlings out* seemed to carry more weight. He had a cleft palate and we couldn't understand a word he said but 'ittle muggers' seemed to feature regularly at some stage, and we were in no doubt about his intent. Naturally we still sneaked in - no gain without pain. My dad as a boy got a real belting from his dad when it was reported that he did not salute the Laird, Colonel Balfour, as he passed. He must have been in a more generous mood when he stumbled upon my sister and my cousin Mabel perched on a branch about ten feet off the ground, competing to see who could pee the farthest. They did not hang around to find out. It was very much the 'overlord' and his tenants.

The same John Liddell had an unfortunate experience after a night at the *sillocks*. A rather gruff individual, not generally known for his sense of humour, he would not have seen the funny side in the way that we did. It just so happened, as the small boat, complete with the evening's catch arrived back at the slipway at Shapinsay pier, it was getting dark, and there was a lobster box lying just off the point at precisely the same level as the slip. In his normal confident almost aggressive style, and with the pronouncement 'Terra firma again', he launched himself over the gunwale of the boat, stepped on to the box and went clean out of sight. It was not the sort of event that people in Shapinsay tend to forget, and many would have given a week's wages to have seen it.

Terra firma

Stories like that were always part and parcel of evenings with relatives as there was no TV, and the wireless only allowed on when the 'man of the house' wanted to hear the news. This we were told was to preserve the accumulator, which powered the set.

'The Gardens' was a fascinating cottage containing a large kitchen which led into a sitting room complete with a box bed. Then you passed out into a flagstone corridor, on past the bedroom and into the *ben* end - all in a row. *Ben* was the best room and contained a carpet, a three-piece suite and a piano. The smell of a log fire in there was great. The house was set in the middle of a large plantation, which caused a minor problem. The 'loo' was outside, situated about fifty yards into the woods. It was a cold, eerie trip in the dark with a torch and a newspaper - usually *The Press and Journal* - to that small closet with its wooden box containing a bucket. Much later it was upgraded to a chemical toilet. Nevertheless, the wind howling through the trees on a *coorse* winter's night was a great laxative, which was a big help when you did not want to linger there a moment longer than you had to.

The gardens with their large greenhouses and high walls yielded much more than the normal Orkney garden. Fresh fruit such as apples, peaches, and grapes were regularly produced. We even sickened ourselves on raspberries, which grew in a small corner of the woods just outside the garden wall where cuttings had been thrown out and had taken root. Peacocks wandered freely about the grounds. The whole place, castle and all, which we were only allowed into later when visitors' days came into being, was a bit of a fairyland to us. Sometimes, if there were relatives up from the south staying at the cottage, we were taken by John Liddell around certain parts of the 'private' grounds, including the lovely 'Ladies Walk' with its colourful flower beds, not a weed in sight, and grass verges as straight as a gunshot.

My best mate in the village was Billy Thompson, better known to his school contemporaries as 'Tompo'. We roamed the village, pier and shore area, played in boats, shared the occasional five Woodbines and generally had a great time. He was a lad of many talents, particularly interested in music and dance, and he eventually progressed to setting up his own highly rated dance school in Edinburgh. There was more to Bill, however, than music and dance; he could run like a whippet, certainly the fastest thing over one hundred yards that I knew in Shapinsay, and there were quite a few excellent sprinters there at that time. I also watched him taking a bee's

Slipway and 'loo' - Balfour village

nest apart with his bare hands so that we could get at the honey. Again, sillock fishing and catching crabs were the big things, and once we managed to get a large lobster ashore with a boat hook, which was considered to be a great achievement.

We always had access to at least one rowing boat and many an hour we spent in Elwick Bay, and rowing round the back of Helliar Holm, the small island nearby. Rowing round the bay or over to Helliar Holm pier on a calm summer's day was really enjoyable. The water rippling round the bow and the birds singing were about the only sounds you could hear. To get round the back meant crossing a reef. At low tide there was only a narrow passage through which the boat had to be navigated, by aligning it between two fixed points; the old gasometer, near the village and the Mull Head in Deerness. At the back of the Holm there were caves to row into, a small sandy cove to swim in, and cliffs to climb. Going into a cave, the water was crystal clear, though deep. As you eased your way in using an oar or your hands on the walls of the cave, you could see everything in the water and on the seabed; fish, crabs, sea urchins, even the occasional lobster.

The island itself was a popular place for picnics and swimming, the only inhabitants being the lighthouse keepers. If you couldn't swim or were only just beginning, you could have had, as I did, the privilege of being thrown over the side of the small pier with a rope tied round your waist. Amazing how your swimming improved, and then you progressed to the main pier at Shapinsay with clear, deep water and plenty of places to dive from. Swimming under water was a big attraction. We had no goggles, snorkels or other equipment, but a big intake of air and down you went and sometimes you came up with something interesting like a live *scarman's head.* This was not something we did too much in Kirkwall Basin, the visibility being somewhat limited.

Fishing along the edge of 'The String' in a rowing boat was fruitful, but tended to be a bit hazardous if you were not familiar with the tides, or, as we did on one occasion, you lost an oar. Luckily, our 'skipper' Tommy Kemp, brother of the late Dave Kemp, was an expert 'sculler' with one oar over the stern of the boat and, thanks to his sterling efforts, we managed to recover the oar just a few feet from the rocks below the lighthouse. We finally made it back to Shapinsay pier about two o'clock in the morning where the reception awaiting us was, to say the least, unforgettable. Even the coastguards had been alerted.

My father's boat was often in Shapinsay during the holidays. We sailed it from the shore below Work Farm, where it usually lay, across 'The String' at slack water. It came in very handy for making an extra bit of pocket money when some officer from the camp behind the Gatehouse wanted to take his wife on a trip round the bay or over to Helliar Holm. This was not with parental approval but the money was good. Usually it was spent on lemonade, sweeties or five Woodbine from the Post Office, which we hid on a ledge down on the shore. The Air Sea Rescue launches berthed in Elwick Bay were spectacular to watch at full speed, and if you were lucky enough to get a trip on one, it was just fantastic.

It was not unusual to take family friends to Shapinsay. On one occasion we accommodated five members of the Firth family along with the four of us; nine of us packed into a 12-foot dinghy. It certainly set the boat down in the water a bit. The two Dads did the rowing and the rest of us squeezed in wherever we could. We had a great day out and made the return journey later the same evening. This sort of escapade requires a good knowledge of the tides in the area. As usual, bicycles were shared for the trip from Eastbank to Work and back.

Shapinsay – here we come

Jean Harrold also came over with us for the day and she made quite a splash when she managed to fall between boat and jetty. It was as well it happened on the return journey or it would have been a long damp day.

'The Smithy' was another interesting place in the village. The bellows, the flying red hot sparks, the noise, the smell of burning hooves, and watching Peter Miller, the blacksmith, effortlessly controlling the big restless farm horses, all added to the atmosphere. A juvenile audience was no problem to him and we were often allowed to pump the bellows while he fashioned a piece of metal into a horseshoe or something on his anvil.

Returning to the subject of toilets, the most interesting 'loos' in Orkney must be the ones near the slipway in Shapinsay. They were two adjoining stone-built cubicles, with seats that hung out over a six feet drop to the shore, one for men and one for ladies. They had no doors but they were well ahead of their time as they were flushed twice a day by the tide. Undoubtedly the thought of visiting one of them at high tide with a strong easterly gale blowing delayed many a visit.

South Brecks, my grandfather's farm, where my cousins Billy and Isobel lived, and the main resort for me, was brilliant. 'Granda' met us with the cart or gig, transported us the two miles or so to the farm, sometimes via the lower road and up the 'thorny ditch', but more often in past the South School, the Old School and the Kirk. Once in the house he usually crushed my shoulder or knee with his enormous hands, smiled, and grunted a couple of words that were intended to be welcoming, and I became 'Dunto' for the duration of the holiday. Most of the time he roared and *goustered* every time we were in sight, apparently always doing something that displeased him. I learned later, however, that he had been afflicted with more than his share of bad luck during his lifetime, and also suffered cruelly from arthritis, so maybe he was entitled to be *crabbit*. Other than that we had no limitations imposed upon us.

The set-up at Brecks, like most farms, was affected by the war, which covered most of the years I spent there on holiday. My Uncle Willie was called up and was away from the farm for most of those years. Presumably my grandfather, who at that time was not all that old, was considered able enough to run the place on his own. In truth, his health was not that good and the bulk of the work had to be carried out by Aunt Chrissie and Uncle John, who was still a teenager. In line with practice elsewhere, however, help was available at busy times like harvest from the various servicemen who were stationed on the island, and who had become regular visitors to the house. Some of them were experienced hands and those who were not were willing to try. We were allowed to join in, though we were probably more a hindrance than a help, and of course at the end of the day there was always enough energy and time left for games, everyone taking part.

My cousin Billy and I were great buddies. We spent a lot of time together during school holidays at Brecks, and then later, when he came to Kirkwall to pursue his secondary education, he stayed with us. He was three years older than me and certainly we both had other pals at that time, but the bulk of our leisure hours we spent together as we were both interested in the

Brecks

same things - football, swimming, gymnastics, the BBs, woodwork and other crafts. I remember us both being introduced to the techniques of French polishing by my Dad, when he was making a doll's crib for one of the family.

At Brecks we ran freely around the farm and surrounding area. We got in many a scrape together but even though we had our moments I cannot remember us ever having a serious fall out. For a number of years we were more like brothers than cousins. He was an athletic lad and I had considerable difficulty in keeping up. I certainly never got anywhere near his ability to run. One thing we were encouraged to do at Brecks was box. There were two sets of boxing gloves in the house and the only rule imposed was that he was not allowed to hit me back, only to defend himself, which for me was great. He did get some of his own back later when he came to Kirkwall to stay, where parental control was less strict. He was a big miss when he completed his education and went back to Shapinsay.

Perhaps I should mention the toilet facilities at Brecks too, since they were vital. The first trick was to find the 'loo'. For some reason it was never in the same place twice running, so, in case it became urgent, you had to establish where to go in a hurry. It flitted regularly between the *neep* shed, the *tattie* house, the coal house, the calfie byre and other such 'suitable' places. As a piece of furniture it was a similar arrangement to that of the gardener's cottage - most farms and country houses had the same set-up at that time - but with less privacy. There was a

cousin up from Edinburgh on holiday with a rather genteel young friend who was clearly unused to *thunderboxes* as we knew them, and no doubt the 'facilities' came as something of a surprise. Nothing like the surprise she got when a *clucker* took exception to her presence, and pursued her as she fled, petrified, out through the *tattie* house door in an embarrassing state of undress. Somewhere in Edinburgh there is a lady who, I am sure, will still remember this experience with some amusement - not too many hens guarding 'loos' down there, *cluckers* or otherwise.

Perils of a country loo

In good weather the whole south end of the island was our oyster. On bad days the barn bore the brunt of our enthusiasm - probably the thing that annoyed Granda most, as our activities tended to knock the oats off his sheaves. Barns must have been designed as secondary playgrounds, although they were hard and uncompromising with flagstone floors and stone walls. If you tripped or made a miscalculation, you knew about it. Swinging hand-over-hand along the couples from the sheaf door to the far end where the threshed straw was piled was a great achievement. There was usually a 'climbing' rope half way along to slide down if you were struggling, but beyond it there was no reprieve and a hard landing awaited if you did not make it. Dropping between the couples into the straw was another trick, and if you could squeeze in a somersault on the way down, so much the better. The less straw the more chance you had, but you had to be prepared for a harder landing. 'Flaying-the-cat' was another acrobatic activity - a sort of somersault while hanging upside down from a couple of ropes.

Even the mill itself offered its attractions - burrowing among the *chaff* (and mice) in the *chaffy house*, or rolling round the big spiked drum that threw out the threshed straw and squeezing into the space behind. Hide-and-seek took on a new meaning when Granda's stick was heard approaching the door. When he came in, glowering round suspiciously, he was totally unaware that he was being watched by four or more pairs of eyes, hidden behind the sacks that hung above the *fanners*, peering out from under the straw, down from the couples, or other such places of concealment. Threshing days were fun, however, and the only time the old man ever did anything with us. We had the job of forking sheaves up to him - they had to be laid the right way round on the sheaf board - and he fed them in, while my Uncle John had the job of clearing the threshed straw from the other end. We had to be kept an eye on, for the mill was operated by a pulley and belt system from the engine shed next door, and there were other moving parts that could have been dangerous.

Outside the possibilities were endless. A couple of old bikes added to the fun. Though intended purely for transport they came into their own in places like the stack yard, where we raced round the narrow spaces between stacks hoping that no one was coming the other way, or that a pedal did not catch in a stack net - something which happened frequently. Bumps and bruises were an accepted part of the fun. Sliding down planks laid up against a stack, draped in a *tattie* sack to protect us from potential splinters, was our version of a chute. There was a burn between Brecks and the neighbouring farm of Hannatoft, which was little more than a large, deep ditch, but wide enough to build an impressive dam, forming a fairly substantial paddling pool. One slight problem arose when a German bomber, having been warned off its intended target by the Orkney defences, ditched its bombs over Shapinsay and one, which did not explode, was embedded in a field alongside 'our burn'. We had to stay away from this area until it was defused.

The small quarry above the farm, basically intended for watering the horses, yielded many a soaking. An old wooden washtub was our favourite raft but it was a notoriously unstable thing and soakings were guaranteed at almost every attempt. It was not deep, but when you went in head first you got pretty wet. The final indignity for me was plummeting head first over Queen, the big white farm horse's head, when I forgot to let go her mane as she bent down for a drink. I don't know who got the bigger fright, her or me. The deep quarry above the manse was 'out of bounds', and in the main we did stay away from it.

The *ipery* ditch running from the stable, byre and pigsty, down the slope at the end of the house, was something of a challenge. It had to be crossed to get to a favourite play area, the *brecks*, after which the farm was named. It was possible to clear it with a decent jump but this did not always happen, especially if you were trying to convey someone else across on your back. Two smelly bairns take more cleaning up than one. For many years after the event I was reminded of the time when I dropped my younger cousin Isobel into the ditch, all dressed up in

Dam builders

summer frock, white ankle socks and new white plimsolls. Apparently, I had covered the good half-mile to the Old School heading for refuge with relatives in the village when Aunt Chrissie caught up with me, assuring me that everything was 'all right'. It was easy to know when you were not in the good books at Brecks as you suddenly became *min* - 'Git oot o' that min', or 'behave yursel min'. Things were not good when you were reduced to *min*; it was a sure indicator that you were treading on thin ice.

Oops, sorry!

This brings me to an incident which took place when the various ponds and wet areas around the farm were frozen over. My Uncle John watched us sliding on the ice all day, but of course being a teenager he was far too big to join us. The following morning, however, when we went out to continue our fun we found his cap, complete with a packet of fags inside it, frozen to a big crack in the ice. He wasn't at his best that day.

The minister from the manse just above Brecks quite often came down to visit, which suited us fine as he regularly instigated fun and games; hide and seek, *picco*, offers and catchers, rounders, football and so on, with as many as a dozen all joining in including the grown-ups, some of the visiting servicemen and the dog. Hide-and-seek was especially good on a farm. At Brecks, with the house out of bounds, there were still eight outhouses, ten if you included the duckie house and the pigsty, all offering a variety of 'hidey holes', and outside there were two carts, several stacks, dykes, the garden, the mill course, the pond, and several hen houses. Hiding from a person was not difficult, but to get away from 'Pup' the collie was not so easy.

There was always a dog to play with, invariably a collie. Mac, the old dog at Brecks, which had been an excellent farm dog, was getting past it, but Pup was always full of beans and ready for games at any given time. One game, which we learned, involved swapping seats, while the person in the middle, armed with a rolled-up newspaper whacked as many bottoms as he or she could before we all got re-seated. On one unfortunate occasion I had forgotten that I had a boil on my behind until it got severely whacked. It took a lot of the enjoyment out of that particular game - the thought of it makes my eyes water yet. In amongst all this mayhem we also collected wildflowers, seashells, and made 'scent' from water and rose petals. We had a softer side.

Ministers, as a rule, were held in some awe. They were not all like the one who organised the games for us, and when a 'visitation' was made, especially if it had not been intimated, it caused a bit of panic when he arrived. Everybody had to be on their best behaviour. A young couple, home on holiday from *the Sooth*, were in Shapinsay for the day and, true to tradition, Sandy and his wife visited each household in turn. A welcoming refreshment was offered at every house as they went which Sandy happily consumed, more happily as the day went on. His stop at one particular place coincided with an unexpected visit from the local cleric, who was seen arriving just in time. Sandy was ushered into the bedroom and warned severely to stay there and remain silent. All went well through the visit; the informal chat, the cup of tea, even the prayer, but unfortunately the minister suggested a verse of *The Old Rugged Cross* before he departed. On the start of the second line, a powerful but not all that tuneful voice joined in from the bedroom. Sandy had to be produced in all his glory and the necessary excuses had to be made. On his departure, I doubt if the overriding feeling in the house was as the minister would have liked it to have been.

On another occasion the farm dog let the side down. He normally lay under the large kitchen table when the family was having their midday meal, hoping for scraps to be passed down, but for some reason he was not there when the minister dropped in unannounced. He was offered a seat at the table, but unfortunately during the meal the man of the house inadvertently broke wind, not noisily but it was not something that could easily be ignored. In an attempt to retrieve the situation, 'father' kicked out with his foot, shouting, 'Git oot o' here ya stinkan brute', but of course, there was no dog. His embarrassment forced him to blot his copybook further by declaring, 'that bloody dog's never here when it's wanted'. I doubt if ministers hold that kind of sway any more.

Seasonal occupations, which were a necessary chore to those on the farm, were just more fun to us *Toonies*. We followed the horse-drawn reaper, making bands and tying sheaves. We carted sheaves on a sled pulled by one of the two white horses, with us perched on top. It amused us no end when the load got caught while rounding the corner of the house and slid off - not considered at all funny by 'Granda'. We helped to build stacks and chased after mice when the *stooks* were dismantled. Even singling *neeps* and gathering *tatties* all seemed great fun when you did not have to do it. We chapped neeps and went for the cattle at milking time, usually with one of the farm dogs to keep order. We tried milking by hand - not very successfully; 'separated' milk in the separator to extract the cream for making cheese and butter; fed calves, cattle, pigs, hens, and gave milk to lambs with a bottle. We didn't feed the horses, they were just too big. We gathered eggs and hunted for nests outwith the henhouses, watched chickens being hatched in a 'brooder' and we went up to the well for water, two buckets full, which were kept clear of the legs by a wooden frame. Even this offered some fun as you tried to swing a full bucket of water in a circle from the knee up over the head and down again without spilling a drop - it was possible but not always achieved. The tasks were endless. No wonder we slept like logs at night, comforted by a supper of new warm milk and Flett and Sons *coarse biscuits* covered in farm butter. Off we went to bed with an oil lamp, a hot water bottle or *pig*, checking that the *chanty* was underneath for emergencies.

Carrying home the water

Sleeping two in a single bed, even in a crib occasionally when turning over had to be done in unison, or three in a double bed, was often essential, but it all added to the fun. One hot water bottle between two, or worse three, caused some ripples at times, but once you buried yourself well into the *chaffy bed sek* you soon warmed up, especially if you were the middle one of three. On occasions, when the *bed sek* had been newly filled with *chaff*, a certain amount of consternation and hilarity would occur during the night when it was discovered that a mouse had inadvertently been included. Sleep was out of the question until the 'visitor' was caught and disposed of.

Mouse hunt

At least eleven people could be accommodated comfortably at Brecks using all available space; five in the bedroom and boxroom off, two in the *ben* end, two in the attic and the one who drew the short straw in beside 'Granda'. There was no horsing about or idle chat there, that's for sure, and he snored like a drain.

As in most country parishes, Shapinsay schoolchildren had harvest holidays, which we envied, but for them it just meant more hard work.

One of the fascinating discoveries made about Brecks was that from the *ben* end you could crawl under the box bed, continue under Granda's bed into his room (provided he was not there) and climb the ladder outside his bedroom door into the attic, which was partly floored. From there, you could scramble out over the couples of the *but* end ceiling, drop down into the scullery, and climb through a small 'borrowed light', which brought you into the box room, off the bedroom at the opposite end of the house from where you started. All this was managed only having passed through one door. We made this journey regularly, ending up covered in cobwebs and fluff but filled with a great sense of achievement.

Something else common in farmhouses was the number of flies, bluebottles, *clegs*, etc that buzzed around the house. This was due to the presence of livestock and a 'midden' nearby. They were attacked with sticky flypapers, which after a time were covered in hundreds of little corpses before being replaced by a fresh one. This progressed to cardboard parrots, impregnated with DDT, which stunned or killed them when they went near. As they were usually attached to the lamp it was not uncommon to be sitting at the table having dinner, when there was a 'plop' alongside, or if you were unlucky, in your plate, made by a dropping insect.

We also had our own 'private' beach, a small area of shingle among the rocks just below *Osted*. Sometimes we set off on our own down the 'thorny ditch' or across the fields, but at other times when there was a rare slack day on the farm, a picnic was organised with all sorts of home-baked scones and cakes, which were washed down with glasses of milk. The rocks on the left of the 'pool' were just high enough to dive off when the tide was in. Swimming *cossies* or *dippers* were something else. Before progressing to a personal *cossie*, there was available a selection of full length outfits, navy blue with white trim, which had, as far as I can remember, three inch legs and arms, and which were all one adult size. We were installed in one of those, and after lots of *tooks* and tying of knots, necessary to make it fit, you were away. On occasions, when for some reason - like recovering from measles or something - we had been warned to stay out of the sea, we had to swim in the 'buff', and then run along the banks until dry. This lost a bit of its charm when we discovered once that we were being observed by two young ladies from the nearby farm.

Pre-bikini 'cossie'

Shopping meant a trip to Willie Burr's, or more often Astley Cottage, which tended to take hours even though they were only a couple of fields away. We had to go over the 'hill' (little more than a bump but it seemed huge at the time) to Astley. At certain times of the year we looked for four-leaved clovers, collected heather berries and ate them, or if there were enough we took them home and my aunt made jam. Shop vans were also part and parcel of country life and it never failed to amaze me the amount of goods that could be packed inside, outside, or on top of a relatively small vehicle. Everything from bars of chocolate to paraffin was available. Often, the van man would trade his wares for fresh eggs, which helped to keep the bills down.

Being a country shopkeeper calls for a high degree of tact and delicacy if valuable customers are to be kept. A young girl, working in a shop in Shapinsay, noticed a female customer slipping someone else's butcher meat into her shopping bag. At that time, a lot of the meat consumed on the island came out from Kirkwall and was supplied to meet specific orders. Not sure what to do, she went through to the house and mentioned what had happened to her father. His instructions were to stay in the house and ignore him when he shouted her name. He then went through, said good morning to the customer, and busied himself tidying shelves. After a moment, he called the girl's name, but got no reply. After several further unsuccessful attempts he went over to the counter and with a comment about young people not attending to their work, he emptied the lady's bag saying, 'What has she gaen you today Mrs .... Oh dear, she's gaen you the wrong butcher meat,' laid the offending parcel back on the counter and carried on completing her order. With this simple ruse he kept his butcher meat and his customer, and the daughter was off the hook.

Another story goes that a young lad, sent to get some peas, was also instructed to ask for the shopkeeper's wife, who had been ill. It was a fair distance from the shop, and to be sure he did not forget his instructions he repeated them regularly all the way there, 'A pund o' peas and hoo's yur wife? A pund o' peas and hoo's yur wife?' On arrival, the shopkeeper approached him and asked what he wanted today. 'A pund o' peas and hoo's yur wife?' was blurted out instantly. 'Split 'r whole?' asked the shopkeeper? 'Oh my, me mother'll be sorry tae hear that,' was the sympathetic answer. The misunderstanding, however, was soon cleared up, and the boy went home, complete with peas and better news of the shopkeeper's wife. Apparently, there was a blend of tea that was actually called 'One and sixpenny tea', and it tended to cause amusement when the 'man' of the shop shouted through to his wife, 'Hoo much is your wan and sixpenny tea, Isa?' 'Two shullings, Wullie,' was the helpful reply.

On a farm holiday personal hygiene did not have a high priority, partly because the only hot water available had to be heated on the stove, but also because changes of clothes were not all that plentiful, and anyhow there was rarely the time to spare. It added to the 'atmosphere'. There was and still is, although it is different now, a certain aura about a farm, but as older folks would point out there is 'clean' dirt and 'dirty' dirt and a grain o' clean dirt never hurt anyone.

The combination of smells on a farm came from various sources, but there was rarely anything unpleasant about it. What emanated from the byre, the stable, the pigsty, hen houses, and even the 'midden', combined with smells from the barn, wild white clover, newly cut hay and more localised perfumes from nettles, wild mint, the many wild flowers, *neeps, tatties*, peat smoke and baking from the house, made a general 'air' that was familiar on all farms and completely acceptable. We never noticed it. There were no diesel fumes, silage or slurry to spoil it.

Tinklers used to come round, mostly during harvest time looking for extra work and selling dishes, pots and other goods. They usually camped in a tent just above the farm and we visited them from time to time. We were always made welcome.

Another farm, Elwick, owned by my Great-Uncle Mac, was different again. It had a huge mill, which added a whole new dimension to the range of things we did. The farm buildings and house were right on the shore's edge, which was another bonus, apart from the effect it had on duck eggs. I liked duck eggs but I could not cope with the ones at Elwick as the ducks fed mostly on the seashore and their eggs were stronger than any wild bird's egg I ever ate. To me, Elwick had everything. I cannot think of anywhere better to have spent a childhood, even a lifetime. The first things you heard in the morning when you woke up were the sea and the seabirds. You looked out the window, which faced south, and on a spring morning with the sea mist lying on the water and the sun beginning to rise over Helliar Holm, you could hardly wait to get out on the beach or down to the mill pond. Even in rough weather the atmosphere which surrounded the place was great.

The mill was three storeys high, with a rope and hatch arrangement operated by the mill wheel, which went down the middle of each floor, for raising and lowering the oats and meal. For us it also offered a way of moving between the various floors without climbing the wooden stair - not with the blessing of the adults but that just added to the attraction. The huge kiln was a bit scary if you looked down from the top, three floors up, and the whole milling procedure - drying, grinding, bagging, cleaning the metal plates, truing up the grindstones - was fascinating to watch. Apparently, in my Dad's time, it was not an uncommon practice to climb down inside the big mill wheel and 'walk' or run it around, before catching a spoke to get back up to ground level again - not to be recommended. The only occasion on which my sister and I decided to try this was on the old, smaller, wooden wheel. She had to go first and she got on the wrong side of the spoke (as she did with everything). Thanks to a timely rescue by the two farm

Elwick with mill pond

servants, Dave Work and Jock Allan, she was not hurt, but that put paid to any hope I had of trying it. I very early formed the opinion that in mixed families the boy should always be the older. Careful observation has indicated that older sisters get ideas above their station and this frequently leads to trouble.

Another dare at Elwick was to make your way from the duck pond at the shore, up the mill course which went underground for about 75 yards to the mill, with only a box of matches to light the way and scare off the rats. Opening the sluice gate up at the milldam, a job often delegated to us, usually inspired a fruitless attempt to race the water for a distance of about a quarter of a mile, back down to the mill. Trying to lift the big cast iron weights in the mill was another test, and it was a big day when you managed to get a 56lb weight above your head. Uncle Mac could put two up with either hand.

Elwick house was fascinating, with box rooms secreted everywhere, providing sleeping quarters for the servant men and lass. In the closet off our bedroom there were piles of old magazines - the more expensive ones like *Country Life*, *The Sphere*, and others - which gave many an hour's pleasure on wet days. It was an old house with low ceilings, furnished in the style you would expect from a well-off confirmed bachelor, basic in the working areas but with quite a bit of elegance in the best end. He had an organ, which he could play, and he had a good tenor voice. He was also a bit of a wag. A very good friend of mine, Dennis, told me that once, while he was employed at Elwick, Uncle Mac suggested that he took the horse into the sea to cool down after a hard day. What he didn't tell him was that the horse had a habit of keeping straight on regardless of the water's depth - not a happy situation if you were not a swimmer. He had a wicked sense of humour at times. He was a horrendous driver and Dennis got some of his own back when he had the pleasure of towing him out of a ditch with the tractor. He never married, although the indications were that he was well sought after, but being the kind of guy he was he always believed that someone better would come along.

Though we spent a lot of time on the island we only knew about a third of it. We never went beyond Astley unless there was a show, a wedding, or a dance at 'the hall'. Dances and weddings were lively affairs. Invariably, the adult men had a 'wee refreshment' with them which was normally hidden outside in a dyke, a stook, or some other discreet place, and friends were invited outside to partake. After a *tot* or two and a few tins of slipperine scattered on the floor, they were off. I remember on one occasion watching Jook Sinclair, Jim Meason, Sammy Bews and 'Bunny' Bruce, with their wives, doing the 'quadrilles' or the 'lancers'. It was spectacular to say the least and the women's feet hardly touched the floor. The custom for the older men was to play *euchre* in a small room at the back. Undoubtedly, they had their own '*peedie* refreshment' on hand.

The annual agricultural show was a great occasion with the usual gathering of young men passing *halfies* around in some discreet corner, and lots of hilarity and leg-pulling going on. One gentleman, who had an unfortunate speech impediment, was asked what he had in the show that day. 'Hoo hoos and a half', he declared. 'But you can't have half a coo', observed the leg-puller. 'I didn't say half a hoo, I said hoo hoos and a half', (which was intended as 'two cows and a calf'). The debate continued, while we watched amused at the poor man's protestations. Strongmen's games were popular, with sheaves, 56lb weights and other heavy things being thrown about. There were some really strong guys in Shapinsay at that time and the competition was fierce. Races of all kinds were organised and everyone seemed to take part in something.

Hogmanay was great; everyone from the farms around called, usually led by the minister. It amazed us how relatives and friends suddenly went bananas on Hogmanay and New Year's Day. *Home brew* and a *quartie* or *gillick* may have been enough, though a *halfie* would have been the more likely requirement for the festive season. All the cares and worries of the year seemed to vanish. Everyone seemed to be relaxed and happy, laughing, joking, singing, dancing and even playing 'tricks'.

One trick that sticks in my mind was instigated by my Uncle Jim and his mate, Jim Groat, two of the greatest practical jokers I ever knew. The idea was to get us kids to try and slide a sixpence from the forehead, down the bridge of the nose, and drop it into a *filler* tucked in our trouser belts. It was fun, and of course some of the adults expressed an interest, in particular the local minister. He had to have a go. When concentration was at its peak and the 'tanner' almost at the point of dropping off his nose, my uncle tipped a glass of *home brew* into the *filler*, which, as arranged, was tucked inside the top of his *breeks* - enough said! Another regular practice, set up by us, was to have one extra large glass of *home brew* on the tray and when we offered it to a certain gentleman we always made sure that the large glass was as far from him as possible. Without fail he stretched over to get it. All this happened under the watchful eyes of parents, and though we were regularly told off about it, I am sure it amused them as well.

On New Year's Day visitors still came along, but the men also went 'first footing'. I remember being allowed to go out with my Dad and a friend, Bob Sinclair, and as usual they took shotguns with them. Nowadays, this would be considered a crazy thing to do, but it was one of the few days off they had and a good opportunity to add something to 'the pot'. Actually, there was little danger; they were gun-wise, and the alcohol intake amounted to only a few drams or glasses of ale over a long period of time and with long walks between places.

Sundays were different. No work was done on a Sunday unless, like feeding and milking, it was essential. We weren't made to go to church with the grown-ups but we were severely restricted to playing quiet games. Evenings often began with everybody gathered in the *ben* end singing hymns, with my aunt at the organ. As the evening progressed it changed gradually to American folk songs, Scottish songs and even some of the less naughty war songs. Billy, or John, played the melodian or the guitar, someone else had a *shepherd's reed*, and the rest of us made weird noises with combs and paper or clicking spoons, all of us singing like mavises. *The sun shines bright on my old Kentucky home, 'tis Summer the darkies are gay*, was a favourite, conjuring up pictures of young black children playing happily in the cotton fields on long, warm, sunny days. Can't see that going down a bomb nowadays.

Telling stories was another evening pastime and if the stories were true and concerned someone we knew, so much the better. Stories were repeated and enlarged upon regularly until they became part of the lore of the district. One story that was told often concerned an elderly, somewhat disgruntled gentleman. It relates how he used to look at a photograph of his lovely young wife on their wedding day, and then at her elderly, rather portly figure as she sat in a chair, and pointing to the two contrasting images he would bemoan, 'luk at that, and luk at that'. It could not have done much for her well-being and she assuredly had worn as well as he had over the years. Not the most benevolent of men it would seem.

Another tale concerned my mother and her friend Dolly, when going on a visit to old Willie Liddell, the same gentleman who used to chase us out of *the plantings*. They had been well warned not to snigger when he spoke, knowing that he had a cleft palate, and this they promised not to do. As soon as they got in, however, his first question concerned Dolly's dad, who apparently had been unwell. 'And hoo's yur heather, Holly?' ('How is your father, Dolly'), he asked. I don't think he got a reply as they shot out the door.

One deviation from Shapinsay holidays was a fortnight with relatives in Sanday. It was just after the war and it gave me an opportunity to do 'work' that qualified for my BB National Service badge. It also introduced me to the pleasures of 'benty bugs' after a trip on top of a cartload of bent. There was an ENSA concert, which we attended, where the highlight of the show was a tenor singing *'Frinche, frinche, frinche, frinche fa la lala la la'* from *La Danza* by Rossini. It went down well. There was a dance after the show, which was great.

Sanday had a lot in common with Shapinsay apart from one thing - the sandy beaches. The beach below Bressigarth was fabulous. It was a large enclosed bay with a narrow entrance from the sea which at low tide was just a stretch of sand. On a sunny day, with the sun baking the sand before the tide came in, the water, which never became really deep, was very warm, at least by Orkney standards. You could swim there for hours.

Stromness is only a short bus ride away from Kirkwall but it never seemed to feature in holidays for anybody I knew. To us it was as remote as Aberdeen, Glasgow or Edinburgh, and probably mentioned less, as we had relatives in those three cities who visited us on holiday and sent cards at Christmas. We knew nobody from Stromness.

I vaguely remember being in Stromness just before or early in the war, when my Dad and I were given the chance to go in Bertie Rendall's car. Bertie was a joiner who worked with my Dad and who had managed to acquire his own car; not a common possession for a tradesman at that time. I seem to remember there was a boat in the bay made of concrete, which was used for storing coal for the herring fleet, but other than that and the run in the car, I have no recollection of what we saw or did that day. I would not have been in Stromness again until I was a BB of about 12 or 13 years old, when the two companies' football teams met at the Market Green. Many of us were not yet big enough to be considered for the team but we were bussed there to cheer our side on. Strong partisan support was soon evident between the older members of the two camps, which we happily joined in. Mind you, footballers were never as bad as hockey players. Someone I have known for a very long time assures me that the matches between Stromness and Kirkwall Ladies were something else. She still has the scars to prove it.

Following visits would have been to play football, when I played for Kirkwall Rovers' junior team, but as the games at that time were mostly played at Warbeth, a mile or two outside Stromness, those visits added little to what we knew of the town itself. On the two occasions that I went to Hampden to watch Scotland play England we went with the ferry *St Ola*, but we saw little other than the pier, so all in all my knowledge of Stromness before I was a teenager was very sketchy.

Things changed when my sister began to go out with a Stromness lad, who had the good sense to come to Kirkwall to serve his time as an electrician. It was not long before Ronnie invited me out for weekends to his house in Alfred Street, where his Dad also had a shop and a store called Humphrey's. Suddenly a whole new batch of friends became available, and, as in Kirkwall, some with nicknames. There was Sneezy, China, Mugga and Woolfy, whom I already knew slightly as he came to Kirkwall to stay with relatives in the Quadrant where my cousin Arnold lived. There was Charlie, Stromness Athletic's penalty taker supreme, Arthur, Billy Garson, Ronald Smith, and George Brown, better remembered now as George Mackay Brown. George, whose mother was a great friend of Ronnie's Mum, was a regular visitor to the Wilson

Penalty – Charlie style

Stromness

household. In time, he became probably the most famous Stromnessian of all time as a writer of world renown, but when I first knew him he was first and foremost a footballer, and would probably have sacrificed all his later fame to have played regularly for Stromness Athletic, or better still for Glasgow Celtic, his other great love. A great humorist and one of nature's gentlemen, George never changed and once a friend you were always a friend.

Weekends at Ronnie's were great. After work on a Friday night we caught the bus, usually driven by Jake Garson. As he never allowed his bus to go above 30 miles per hour and stopped frequently to drop off or pick up passengers or to deliver parcels, it inevitably took a minimum of three quarters of an hour to cover the 15 miles to the Pier Head.

Saturdays were usually spent playing football with Ronnie's mates at the Market Green, gathering at the Pier Head for a blether, sitting in Norrie Cummings's café, or playing snooker in his billiard rooms. I also got my first taste of golf in Stromness where a lot of the younger lads played regularly. Unlike Kirkwall at that time they were encouraged to join. As a complete rookie I was in no position then to pass an opinion on the quality of the course - to me it seemed a lovely little place.

As in Kirkwall, Sundays were treated with a certain amount of respect. If the weather permitted we usually went for a walk with one or two others up Brinkie's Brae, out to Warbeth beach, or up to the Black Craig, just messing about really. It was not unusual to go to the evening service in the church. On winter evenings we usually stayed at home chatting or playing records on the gramophone.

Monday mornings, unfortunately, meant an early start as we had to catch the county truck - the lorry which collected the county council roadmen. As they started work in Kirkwall at 8am and with lots of stops on the way to pick up passengers, we had to be up at the crack of dawn, which in wintertime was dark and cold. We had to have breakfast - a cooked one, as decreed by Ronnie's Mum - and be out on the street in time for the pick up. The driver did not wait. After being shaken about in the canvas covered back end of the vehicle for at least an hour, you finally arrived in Kirkwall frozen to the marrow and just about hanging on to your breakfast. Still, it was worth it.

All in all I found Stromnessians quite normal - more or less just like us. One thing that I did notice was that in Stromness they talked about 'nails' while in Kirkwall we called them 'nelse'.

They also would say 'the papers were late', but in Kirkwall, 'the pippers were lit'. I suppose they do live farther south than we do. Of course, I frequently have to remind my sister that even though she has lived most of her life in Stromness she is still a Kirkwall Starling. You can keep a nightingale in a henhouse but it is still a nightingale.

The only time I had a holiday south was to join my mother in Edinburgh. She was looking after the family while her sister was having another baby, and it coincided with a BB camp in Aberdeen, which I will touch on later. The plan was for me to take the train from Aberdeen to Edinburgh and be met by someone at Waverley Station, some time around 7pm. By some freak chance the train was early, and having made some enquiries about buses, I decided to make my own way to Cambusnethan Street. This worked fine, but on arrival at the flat after climbing about six flights of

Humphrey's with Ronnie's folks' house at the back

The main street – Stromness

stairs I found a locked door. I decided to go to the Portobello Pool where I thought my cousin, a keen swimmer, might be, but on the advice of a very helpful 'clippie', I got off the bus just outside the park where Meadowbank Stadium now stands. There was a football match on and I watched Meadowbank Thistle beat Musselburgh Union 2-1. It was a good match. On returning to the flat there was still no one home, and by this time I was getting peckish, so I went out and found a nearby chip shop and queued for a fish supper - not as good as Donnie Chalmers' fish suppers, but not bad. At last, when I got back this time, about 10.30 pm, my uncle, who worked as a policeman in Leith, had just arrived home. I will not say what he said but I seemed to have caused a bit of a *toot-fie*. I found all this a bit strange as nobody ever worried about kids being out late in Kirkwall. We always came home when we were ready.

Other than that the holiday was fine. My relations were very good to me, they took me to lots of interesting places - in fact my policeman uncle walked the legs off me - Holyrood House, Edinburgh Zoo, Princes Street Gardens, the Castle, and so on. In the evenings we played games, darts being the favourite. It was also great stepping on and off trams and touring round the city in a bus, but in all honesty, after four weeks of city life, I was ready for home; too much walking, too many people, cars and fumes, too much noise.

The trip home was something in itself. My uncle, who knew Captain Logie of the *St Magnus*, arranged for me to have a bunk in the steerage compartment, right up in the bow of the ship. Maybe he was getting his own back. I was joined by a schoolmate of mine, and 'Beetle' and I kept each other company on the two nights and a day that it took to get home. The first night was the voyage from Leith to Aberdeen and it was rough, and I mean rough. We were rising at least twenty or thirty feet at a time before crashing down again into the next wave. All night long we ploughed our way north, heaving and tossing like something demented. It was one of the longest nights I can remember. After reaching Aberdeen in the early hours we got ashore and wandered round the city looking for something to do. We eventually came to the Bon Accord Street baths, known to me from the BB camp, and as we had no *dippers* we sat and watched the entertainment for a while. Later, we made our way back to the *St Magnus* for sailing out at 5 pm. I avoided my steerage berth and managed to squeeze into a gap between the cooker and a cupboard in the cook's galley, amidships, and even though it was another heavy sea I managed to nod off from time to time. I was glad to be home in the morning.

Although visiting places all over the world is now commonplace, going to locations we had never even heard of, we never felt deprived. Holidays, as we enjoyed them, were brilliant.

Special days and events . . .

Some things never change. The excitement of Christmas or a birthday is as real to children now as it was sixty years ago. There may not have been as much about, but everything is relative and what we were given was just as 'gob-smacking' as anything they get now. Looking at our grandchildren, you can see in their faces the same expectancy as we had. It did not start as early, with Christmas nowadays beginning almost as soon as Easter is past, at least as far as shops are concerned. For us it began sometime in December when the box of decorations was unearthed or the Christmas cards were brought out for writing. Christmas cards were bought from Leonards, individually chosen from trays of loose cards, each tray priced so that you knew which one to select from.

It was a magic time, unpacking the decorations and helping to fix them up. We had two multicoloured ones that were pulled out and strung across the room from corner to corner, supplemented by four two-toned ones that were twisted and pinned up with loops hanging down along the four walls. The finishing touches were added with a paper bell in each corner and a paper star round the light. Real Christmas trees were not to be had and there were no fairy lights, fancy tree decorations or crackers. My sister had a small artificial Christmas tree that I was not allowed to touch, not even to put some cotton wool 'snow' on the branches. It had small candleholders on some of the branches where candles were fitted and lit for short spells. We opened cards and presents as they arrived. We could not possibly wait until Christmas day. On the Sunday before Christmas we went to Sunday school and the kirk to sing carols, and there were usually carol singers from the Girl Guides or Rangers, out on Christmas Eve, that we followed around, sometimes even getting the responsibility for a collection tin.

We wrote our letters to Santa, hung up the biggest stockings we could find on the brass rod and then tried to get some sleep. On Christmas morning we were never disappointed. Santa must have done his homework as we always seemed to get exactly what we wanted, and each item was taken out and studied with great interest. An apple and an orange were always found at the bottom of the sock. Christmas dinner was always a Shapinsay hen, with oatmeal stuffing, dished up with tatties, vegetables and gravy, followed by trifle and real cream and washed down by a glass or two of ginger wine, made by us a week or so before from Abbot's ginger wine essence.

It was very much a family day and the only interruption to playing with toys and games, up until bedtime, was the King's speech on the radio at one o'clock. Everyone sat silently listening to what he had to say, or in our case until he was done. The days that followed were spent playing with new things or visiting friends to see what they had got. It was a sad sort of a day when all the decorations had to be taken down, the Christmas tree that I was not allowed to touch put away, and life got back to normal, before heading for Shapinsay and the New Year. The Christmas cards were kept to cut up for scraps. One particular type of card, quite common, featured 'the hunt', with men in scarlet suits on beautiful horses galloping over the fields. Not knowing what they were galloping after we thought they were great.

Hogmanay and New Year were always part of our Shapinsay holidays, until eventually I was tempted to stay in Kirkwall, when I was invited to take in the New Year at Ardmohr, Bill Sutherland's house (he was my boss at the time). I stayed with the Firths at Eastbank, and cycled between the two houses. My one outstanding memory of that evening was Alfie Walls standing on Dr Sydney Peace's stomach, at his invitation I have to say, just to prove how strong his abdominal muscles were. The return of the boys' ba' completed my move to Kirkwall for the festive season. It restarted in 1945, and I joined the scrum for the first six ba' games, or more accurately, three of them, as the other three were over in a flash. Evan McGillivray ran down to the harbour with the first one, and Peter Baikie raced away with the next two. Most of us hung around the edges of the men's games as well until we were big enough to take a full part. We were not discouraged, and if any of us got jammed in too deeply we were always rescued by some of the older participants.

Easter did not amount to much. We did not roll hard-boiled eggs down hills, and Easter eggs, as much of a treat as they were, were not very big, and were basically just chocolate with artificial cream inside, and, of course, they had to come from your monthly ration. Sometimes you got a small yellow, fluffy, chicken to go with it.

Hallowe'en was much more exciting. We always got a bag of monkey nuts in their shells, and since they were never seen at any other time of the year, they were a special treat. With hands tied behind our backs, we tried to bite apples hanging from the clothes pulley on a piece of string. Even better, we ducked for apples in the tin bath, or better still up at Eastbank, in the big bath. Three or four heads all under water at one time and all searching for a bite was great fun. We did not wear witches' masks or dress up as ghosts, nor did we go out doing 'trick or treat' as they do now. The pranks now played, taking garden gates off or covering door handles with something revolting had not yet started, not in Kirkwall anyhow, or I expect we would have been in there.

Your birthday was the other main event of the year. Apart from the presents -cards did not seem to be so important then - you were made to feel very special. I cannot remember having any big birthday parties, though I do recall being at a few. Three of us, however - Jimmy Firth, Jim Robertson and myself - always went to each other's houses on our birthdays, played together all day and had a birthday meal laid on at teatime. I did arrange my own big party once, inviting at least half the class, but when this was discovered I had to go round and cancel the invitations. It was not surprising - mothers do need a little warning. It was not a complete failure, however, as Charlie Hibbert turned up, complete with present, and we had a great evening. Perhaps I forgot to tell him. *Clootie dumplings*, complete with threepenny bits were the main feature of the birthday meal, and amazingly most of the threepennies seemed to turn up on the birthday person's plate. *Dumplings* were huge and, despite being attacked by some fairly healthy appetites, there was always enough left over for the next day, or even two, when it tasted equally good fried.

Guy Fawkes was a low-key affair during the war. Fireworks and bonfires would hardly have done during the blackout, so unless there was an air raid we had to settle for a few sparklers. Once the war was over things changed considerably. Fireworks and bonfires were very much part of the festivities even though the range of rockets available at first was limited. Sky rockets, bangers of various sizes from penny ones up to thunder-flashes - there were some that you could hold in your hand while sparks flew out of them - and Catherine wheels, were about all there was available to start with. To us they were so exciting we even collected the burnt out remains and kept them for a while.

Uncle John took charge of the fireworks display at Brecks, and on one occasion, so intent was he at keeping us small fry well back he forgot that his backside was hovering over a sky rocket that he had just lit. He did not take off but it was a good job he was wearing a pair of stout trousers. For us, it was the highlight of the evening.

Organised parades began to feature, and we made torches at school under the direction of Alfie Harcus, the woodwork teacher. (He was a Shetlander who had grown up with Up Helly Aa, which may have explained why he knew about torches.) Small ones for small marchers were made from Brasso tins attached to a stick and filled with a rag soaked in paraffin. Big ones were made from whole sacks, wired round a pole and also soaked in paraffin. The torchlight procession marched behind the BB pipe band through the town, with torches blazing, to 'The Crafty'. There, a huge bonfire of wood, old tyres and other combustibles was waiting, and this was set alight by throwing all the torches on top. After the 'Guys' had been judged and prizes awarded, they too were hurled on to the fire. Fireworks, by this time getting more sophisticated, were set off, including flares donated by the coastguards, while the fire-engine stood by in case there were any problems. It made a great evening.

The 'Market', not available during the war, was another welcome addition to the year's events. Set also in 'The Crafty', it started modestly but grew as the years went on, with swing-boats, chair-o-planes, 'rolling the penny' stalls; coconut shies, 'hoopla' stalls with goldfish bowls as the targets; 'housey housey', a shooting gallery and a fortune-teller called Madam Abbey. Johnny Smith's boxing booth came later. We cheated regularly at 'rolling the penny'. We spread around the stall so that the attendant always had his back to someone and that was the opportunity to push your penny on to a square that entitled you to a pay out. We were caught frequently but the rewards made it worth taking the chance. I guess the attendant was used to it and the profits would not have been too bad. Bill Hives's shooting gallery was a popular stall, and we watched Dad Kemp and Busty Findlay competing most evenings for the top prizes. The loud music, the lights, the general 'buzz', made it a great gathering place for the young teenagers of the town, and if you were looking for someone special this was where you were likely to find them.

The Stromness Market was a forerunner of the much bigger 'Shopping Week', which replaced it in 1949. On one occasion five of us decided to go, and as it was a fifteen-mile journey, bikes were our only chance of getting there. We were one bike short so my sister's bike was 'borrowed' - I'm sure she would not have minded - and off we set. Somewhere in the Stenness area the capers got out of hand and a pedal went through the front wheel of her bike. Disaster; a wheel that looked like a figure eight. We half-walked, half-cycled the remaining few miles into Stromness and headed straight for Wishart's cycle shop. It curtailed our spending money as we pooled most of our resources to meet the expected large bill. The day passed fairly quietly until for the first and only time in my life, I had a win at the 'housey housey'; a tea set - great when you are on a bike. At the end of the day, however, we went back to Wishart's fearing the worst, but were absolutely delighted when the bill for two shillings and sixpence was presented, to replace a few spokes. The bike was as good as new, and so, complete with tea set, we headed for home. Next time we went by bus and I remembered to tell my sister about the accident some twenty-five years later.

The County Show restarted in 1946 and it was a big event in the town. At certain times the streets were just as busy as they had been during the war, when there were no shows. From the parishes and islands, everyone who could come, came. The boats were full to capacity and buses were working overtime. Houses were overloaded with friends and relatives, in for the day; for some the only day they left their island all year and Kirkwall Mums worked their socks off to feed them.

Interest in the show varied. The livestock and new farm implements on display attracted the farmers, while the side-shows were of more interest to the *Toonies*. One particular challenge was to retrieve a half crown from a basin full of water. It looked quite simple but the water was electrically charged. Many struggled gamely to get hold of what was a substantial addition to the pocket money, but few succeeded. The pipe band played, there were gymnastic displays put on by us, races were organised for people and ponies, and the beer tent worked flat out all day.

Kirkwall itself was relatively quiet until about four o'clock when things began to wind down at the Bignold Park, and then they came down in droves. People shouted across the street to one another, often pointing to some young lad or lass standing alongside them looking miserable, and posing the dreaded question, 'Dae you ken whaur this is?' Cafés, restaurants, chip shops, any place where there was food to be had, were queued out. The pubs weren't idle either.

Then, during the evening as the boats and buses began to leave town, packed with passengers, the chants of 'Limpets', 'Auks', *'Scooties'*, or whatever, rang out, adding to the atmosphere. The following morning the chip *pokes*, straw, bits of binder twine and the odd empty *quartie* were all cleaned up; the smell of mothballs began to fade and it was all over for another year.

North Isles trip days were important too. Each island had its own separate excursion to Kirkwall and it made for a big day out. The main purpose of the visit was to visit friends or relatives and go to the shops. It brought some welcome additional business to the town, and for some it was the only time they left their island during the year. At the end of it all, as the boat left, the same chanting and waving took place.

One elderly relative, not a grandparent but of that generation, came in from one of the North Isles from time to time. Everybody enjoyed his company, and so did I, with one reservation. My bed provided the only spare space for male relatives and from previous experience I knew that I was in for a poor night. His snoring was something else; not a regular up and down sort of

St Magnus Cathedral

racket that you might get used to, but more of a collection of snorts, grunts, whistles and blasts, not in any particular order, with the outflow making as much noise as the intake. It was like sleeping with the angel Gabriel. He had to catch the early boat, which meant getting up about five o'clock in the morning, and of course my bed was in the living room/kitchen. Everybody apologised for the disturbance in the morning, but in truth it was a blessed relief as at least I could squeeze in a couple of hours' sleep before school. I doubt if anyone in the house got a wink of sleep before then.

Long night

Visitors regularly arrived from the islands or from the *Sooth*. With my father being one of twelve and my mother one of six, with many of the siblings no longer living in Orkney, there was a lot of 'to-ing and fro-ing' all summer. We acted as a sort of 'transit billet', since most of them were on their way to, or from, Shapinsay, where both sets of grandparents lived. We met them off boats, off the *Ola* bus, and off the BEA bus. It was always a mortifying affair meeting them on Broad Street, as every aunt seemed bent on the revolting habit of kissing you. I can still smell the powder and taste the lipstick that you were *clarted* with. Other than that they were fine, at a distance. If there were cousins with them to play with, that was different.

With visitors in mind, when we went out of the house for anything the door was never locked and usually a note was left to say when we would be back. Even when we were on holiday the key was always left under the front door mat in case any friends or relatives needed in to make a cup of tea or go to the 'loo'. They all knew the key would be there. Windows were never locked. There was nothing to steal.

Orkney weddings were another great social event. The church ceremony was always solemn, as it should be, but the festivities that followed made an Orkney wedding different. My early experiences of weddings were all in Shapinsay, mostly in 'the hall', but on the one occasion, when my Aunt Dorothy married Alec, an RAF lad from Edinburgh who was stationed in Shapinsay for part of the war, it was held at Brecks. It was fabulous; music, dancing, singing, everyone having a great time, with the odd *home brew*, or a dram to keep it going well into the small hours. The food, all home-made, was excellent as well.

Weddings in the hall were also brilliant. The food, speeches, music, and most of all the people and their determination to enjoy themselves and to make sure that everyone else enjoyed themselves too, were just amazing. Again, the older men played *euchre* in a small room at the back. It all lasted well through the night, and as a child you were totally caught up in the whole business.

Sundays should be added here as they were always considered to be special days. When we were smaller, Sunday afternoons in summer, provided the weather was good, were usually spent on going for picnics or for walks - long walks. *Traipsing* all the way out to Carness, across the track between fields to Blackhall, and back via Waterfield to Kirkwall, was a favourite, a distance of about four-and-a-half miles. We did not think too much about it once we were underway as there was always plenty to do on the way, scratching about on the shore, making daisy chains, eating wild berries or other delicacies found on the way, playing games or just chatting.

Another 'favourite' walk, which did not appeal so much to the younger fry, was out to the cemetery at Orquil where we wandered amongst the gravestones, picking out names here and there before continuing round Scapa, which was much better, and then back to town. Short legs did get tired and the next proposed 'walk' was always met with dismay, but go we had to and it usually turned out fine.

Later, for a number of years, Sundays were very much church orientated. We started Sunday school more or less when we started day school, under the supervision of Mr Leask, the KGS headmaster. There were various classes organised by age, and each one had a 'teacher'. We had lessons from the Bible, and were issued with copies of *Sunny Stories*, a small magazine, from time to time.

When you were old enough to join the BBs, your day started earlier with the BB Bible Class at

10.15 am, held in the Congregational Church. After Bible Class, as we were going to Sunday school anyhow, we usually went to the Cathedral service as well. This took up the whole morning. Another later addition was the Youth Fellowship, which was begun in the Congregational Church by Mr McCorkindale. He was a really wonderful man, not big, but with a big heart and a great manner with young people, and we crowded into his church every Sunday evening. He would give us a very informal talk about something directly relating to young people, then we would sing Sankey hymns, sometimes getting a solo from Rosemary Muir, and had a break half way through for a mug of tea and a 'jammy piece'. It was nothing big, but on a winter's evening it offered a place for young people to get together, off the streets, at a time when gathering places were few.

Sunday afternoons were 'clear' and we usually patrolled the streets in groups, some boys, some girls, some mixed, just fooling around really. There were no shops open and apart from us kids the streets were more or less deserted. On bad days we crowded into the Central Café, consuming hot oranges, coffees, or other warm beverages under the eagle eye of Mr and Mrs Zanre. The back area was divided up into cubicles with bench seating, which held about six, or even eight, in each space. Not too much hilarity was allowed but like all kids, when together, we had plenty to talk about. We did discover one annoying activity, which was making small paper 'darts' out of sweetie wrappers, wetting them and ejecting them upwards at the ceiling where they stuck fast to the glass panels. I think we spent enough, however, to make up for any nuisance we caused.

Organised sports . . .

Organised sports have not changed that much. Obviously, the facilities now are much better with flood-lit pitches and running tracks, swimming pools, games halls, the leisure centre, proper gymnasiums, squash courts and so on, and there is a wider choice available to young people. Rugby, cricket, squash and volleyball were not played at all in Orkney in our time, but tennis was popular with two courts available at Costie's and one at the Earl's Palace. The tennis clubs that were formed were well supported.

Football for boys, hockey and netball for girls; swimming, golf, if you could afford it and were 'acceptable', bowls if you were 'cracking on a bit' and not fit to play anything more active, were the main summer sports. Gymnastics and badminton were the popular options during the winter. Most of us took part in at least one of them. Lack of proper facilities did not deter us. We had access to what was available at the time, and though comparisons are difficult to assess, the indications are that the standards achieved in the sports we played, during and just after the war, were at least as high as they are now.

Halls of various types were used; church and school halls, the town hall, various huts that remained, and even one of the hangars at Hatston, mainly for badminton. There were several badminton clubs in Kirkwall alone; the St Magnus Club, the Paterson Church Club, the Victoria Club, the Kirkwall Club, the Congregational Club, as well as the King Street Church Club, and the MCA (Ministry of Civil Aviation), who played in the hangar at Hatston. They all competed in the local leagues. My only experience of it, prior to joining St Magnus Club some years later, was a visit to the Paterson Club at the invitation of John Mainland, who worked at WHB Sutherland's at the same time as I did. I enjoyed it, and went to see the open tournaments when I could get a ticket. On semi-finals and finals nights, tickets were like gold, as they were for the inter-county matches with Shetland; and though the crowds were necessarily smaller, the atmosphere during a tight match was electric, and the result taken just as seriously as it was for football or hockey.

Golf was not for kids, being reserved for bankers, doctors and businessmen. Bowls were for older people, mostly men, but we did spend a lot of time watching them, sure in our own minds that we could have done much better.

The main summer sport for boys was football. We began in the backyards, the playground and on the streets, mostly with an old tennis ball, and graduated to playing in school house teams, the BB or Scout teams, then junior club teams (up to the age of 18), and finally, to 'B' or 'A' club teams. Inter-house matches were not all that plentiful and the BB team rarely played more than one game a year, usually against Shapinsay or Stromness, but occasionally against a visiting BB company who happened to be camping in Orkney. (I remember we 'thrashed' the Leith BBs 2-0.) KGS played annual football and hockey matches against Stromness Academy.

Official matches were only part of it, however, and every evening that the weather allowed, games were 'organised' in the Bignold Park on what was the old hockey pitch. Someone produced a ball, teams were formed, with no limit to numbers, and we played until it was dark. We did our own refereeing, which caused the occasional problem, but it rarely developed into a fight.

With so many servicemen here, club football was at an all-time high in Orkney during the war, and when our lads came back, many of them had widened their football experience in other places. I mentioned the Italians, but though they had some brilliant players they only played 'friendlies'. The Camerons and the RAF had teams for a time, but the only essentially non-local club, which played regularly in all our competitions for a number of years, was Hatston, the camp on the outskirts of town. They had some cracking players, a few of them professional. The normal pitch for league matches was in the Bignold Park, though Hatston always had their own pitch. In 1947, however, while the Bignold was getting a major overhaul, Papdale was where we played, in a field now covered in housing, just above where the school pitches are now.

Interest, particularly immediately after the war, was enormous; it was a sort of 'letting the hair down' again after all the worry and hassle. Crowds in excess of 4,000 were not uncommon almost every night of the week, to watch 'A', 'B' and even junior teams in action. All round the pitch, two or three deep, with extra behind each goal, they cheered and shouted with great exuberance. Rivalry was strong and feelings ran high at times. During one particular match between Rovers and Thorfinn, the referee walked off during a brawl and left the players to sort things out for themselves. Local newspaper reports by 'Cubbie Roo', 'Corinthian' and 'Spike' ran into pages and helped to keep the excitement going.

Some training was done in the winter, in a hall, or in the case of the hockey girls, in one of the hangars at Hatston. (This proved to be a bit dodgy, as the hard hockey ball came off the walls and concrete floor like a bullet.) We were lucky to have Willie Brown as coach, who played regularly for Preston North End when they were one of the top sides in England. He spent many of his holidays in Orkney as he was married to an Orcadian girl. Willie was a first class coach.

Inter-counties against Shetland were 'big time'. Every year, hundreds of supporters came down from Shetland, or Orcadians went up there, and a real festival atmosphere took over. Even the shops shut for the duration of the game. Over 5,000 watched, and the result was either a disaster or a great triumph, depending on whom you supported.

Hockey did not get the same benefits from the war as football did, even though there were a lot of women posted to the islands in the various services. I don't think they ever formed a hockey team, nor did any of them play for local clubs. Orkney hockey developed on its own. Hockey club matches and inter-counties, however, followed a similar pattern, with intense interest in all levels of the game. There was one occasion when a visiting team, including several Scottish international players, came to Orkney but only managed to draw 2-2. It was an impressive performance by the local girls.

Playing football for a club team was a big step forward and we often had to travel to the country to play Deerness, Holm, Stromness, Tankerness and Dounby. Playing on some of these pitches had additional hazards. Cow pats and rabbit holes abounded, and, on one occasion, when we were playing against Holm juniors on the island of Lamb Holm, the wind was so strong that we were almost afraid to kick the ball in case it ended up in the sea. Not a lot of atmosphere on that occasion, as we did not have a single spectator.

Snags of a country football pitch

Something that was always done at junior level, when entertaining or visiting one of the 'out of town' clubs, was to lay on a meal afterwards for both teams. It was considered common courtesy, and it helped to foster good relations between players, even if they had been kicking lumps out of one another during the match. We also went to Shapinsay as a junior team, and once, when the boat had broken down and could not take us back to Kirkwall, we were all accommodated most hospitably in various houses around the island.

The Parish Cup was another competition, restarted in 1946, which was ardently supported, as one can imagine. Rivalry was strong at every game and the atmosphere at the final, held in Bignold Park, normally on County Show night, was amazing. I remember sitting on top of the Harray team's bus after they had won the cup, driving through the parish, waving and cheering to people as we passed by, eventually stopping at Willie Firth's house where a party was soon underway.

The greatest Parish Cup final ever for me was the first year that Shapinsay won it. They were the first island team to do so, and the only one until Westray did it many years later. One of my biggest regrets is that I never played in the Parish Cup, but the rules at that time forbade it. Now, if either parent is born in a parish or island you are eligible, but then, even though both my parents were born in Shapinsay I still could not play for them. Sammy Bews tried to persuade me – nobody would be any the wiser, he said - but we both knew it would never work.

The first trip to Hampden Park, to see Scotland and England playing, was quite an event. Tickets were allocated to the Orkney Football Association, who distributed them as fairly as they could among the clubs. The lucky ones made the epic journey there and back to watch Scotland being beaten 2-0. It was something of an adventure for most of us.

We caught the ferry, *St Ola*, on the Thursday morning from Stromness, about 10.30am, struggled to hang on to our breakfasts off Hoy, lunched on arrival at Scrabster about 3 hours later before boarding a hired bus, with no springs, for the long haul south. We arrived in Inverness in time for tea at a chip shop, and to fill in the time most of us then went to the pictures. Willie Spence, his brother and I, went to see *The Flying Leathernecks*, with John Wayne as the hero. We left Inverness late evening, stopping for food in Perth at an all-night transport café, and then travelled on to Glasgow.

We arrived at Buchanan Street station about 4.30am, and dispersed to our various places of accommodation. As an 'experienced' traveller (I had already been to Aberdeen with the BBs, and then on to Edinburgh to my uncle's house), my instructions were simple. I was to go to Fyfe and McGrouther's hardware store where my uncle worked, and he would see me on to a bus to take me to my other uncle at Corkerhill Road, where I was to stay. That bit worked fine when it came, but Fyfe and McGrouther's did not open until 9am. I tramped the streets of central Glasgow for four-and-a-half hours, with no clue where I was going apart from an address. Eventually, I met two enormous Glasgow 'polis', who seemed to have some difficulty hiding their amusement as I explained my plan of campaign. They pointed me in the right

Helpful 'polis'

direction, however, and after some further tramping I eventually found the store. In time, the staff, including my uncle, began to arrive. All went well after that. The Gorbals looked fine to me at that time of morning - a quiet place.

We assembled the following morning at Buchanan Street and went on the bus to Hampden to join the throng. The police horses intrigued us, leaning into the queues to keep them straight. When entering the stadium, we were totally stunned at the size of the place and the crowd, which exceeded 100,000. We saw some of the match but were probably more amazed at what was happening all around us. We were disappointed with the result but with heads held high we made our way slowly back to the bus. The trip home was similar to the one down, with various food and toilet stops on the way. Old Jim Donaldson and Ralph Fotheringham kept their pipes going time about, all the way, and by the time we reached Scrabster I was green. I could not look at lunch and the trip on the *St Ola* completed the job. It was great to look back on, and obviously I must have been as impressed as the others as I joined the same trip two years later. We lost again.

Football gear deserves a mention. Getting your first pair of football boots was some thrill. They had rock hard toes with the rest not much softer, and to 'break them in' we sat, booted, for hours with feet in the sink. Even after that, blisters were still painful for a game or two. Shin guards were essential to cope with your opponents' toecaps and the vicious leather studs that were hammered into the soles. After the leather wore down they were even worse as the nails showed through - not very pleasant to come up against in a tackle. Footballs were made of thick leather panels and the most famous one in our time was the 'T' ball. When they got wet they weighed a ton and it took a bit of thought to stick your head in front of a ball that was travelling at speed. The leather lace that was used to seal the opening where the bladder went in was another problem. Proper footballs,

New football boots

however, were few and far between. I once possessed a home-made one made by a guy who fancied my sister, and, even though it was not quite round, it was a vast improvement on a tennis ball. It broke windows, which was a drawback. Even while playing for Rovers juniors in the early days we only had about seven jerseys that matched, no socks, and no ball. Before a match we had to depend on our opponents letting us warm up along with them. We still succeeded in winning our league, which was more than the senior team managed to do at that time.

The introduction of the Junior County Sports, in 1947, between Orkney and Shetland, was one of the most exciting things that happened to us. The first one was in Shetland. Too young to even think about taking part at first, we were still caught up in the atmosphere and never missed an opportunity to watch the various athletes and sportsmen and women competing in the trials for a place in the team. Going to Shetland to watch was out of the question, but the results of the various events were known all around the town almost as soon as they finished. When the Shetlanders came down the following year the whole place was buzzing for about three days. We accommodated two of the girls' hockey team which helped to make you feel part of the event. We wore rosettes, red and white *toories* and even unearthed hand rattles, saved from the war. We roared ourselves hoarse with the various chants, such as: 'One two three four, who are we for – Orkney!' In the evenings, the streets were alive with Shetlanders and Orcadians mixing together in groups and the whole thing created a carnival atmosphere over the whole town. We could hardly wait until the day when we would be old enough to take part. It is great that this event has kept going.

Lifeboys and Boys' Brigade . . .

The first Lifeboy uniform I ever saw was worn by Alistair Harrold, who lived across the landing from us. All it consisted of was a square cloth badge, showing a lifebelt, and a flat, sailor-type, cap. When worn with a navy blue jumper, trousers, socks and black shoes, however, the effect was most impressive. I was still too young, but already marking time until the day when I could join. A 'naval' type uniform in wartime, boy o' boy! That day came, and I joined a lot of other young lads from Kirkwall and round about, in the KGS hall. We had various activities, mostly games, organised by our two leaders, Miss Moncrieff, the school music teacher, and Mr Fitch, a sailor stationed in Orkney. The only sign of rank I remember, apart from the two officers, was a lanyard worn proudly by the platoon leaders. We went on parade from time to time, usually with the Boys' Brigade, but occasionally we took part in huge parades, which included not only the youth organisations - Scouts, Cubs, Brownies, Guides, Rangers, Sea Cadets, and Army cadets - but the armed forces as well. We felt like real sailors.

The most notable event I remember was a 'route march' from Broad Street in Kirkwall, out to Scapa beach then all the way around the coast to Waulkmill, a distance of some seven-and-a-half miles. On arrival, we were fed while seated on the banks, and then played on the beach for a while. When ready for home, to our relief, we were ushered on to buses to take us back to town.

Having watched the wide range of activities, and the super uniforms available, promotion to the BBs was eagerly awaited. My first glimpse of BB life was a visit to their old 'club' in North Ronaldsay Terrace when I was still a 'lifeboy'. There were boxing gloves, bugles, and all sorts of

LIFEBOYS - c. 1940

Back row: Albert Zanre; Mack Smith; Ian Swanney; Dod Newlands; Arthur Flett; Jim Wylie; Jim Kemp; Norman Laughton; Gordon Peace

One row down: Colin Macgillivray; Donald Sinclair; Tony Rosie; Hugo Shearer; Bob Muir; John Bews; Bernard Borwick; Jim Scott; John Flett

Two rows down: Ralph Miller; Charlie Hibbert; _____ _____; Jack Donaldson; Philip Stout; Jimmy Firth; _____ _____; George Grant; Jim Robertson; Eric Moodie; Stanley Johnston

Three rows down: Dave Peace; Jack Walker; Tommy Drever; Miss Moncrieff; Mr Fitch; George Donaldson; Alec McEwan; Bruce Dunnet

Four rows down: Cecil Sutherland; Dave Turfus; Jim Sutherland; Self; Billy Sinclair; Jack Sinclair; Brian Turfus; Peter Burgess; Peter Baikie

Front row: Roy Bichan; Tommy Walker; Ian Gray; Oliver Campbell; John Gray; Norman Laughton interesting stuff lying around, plus a most impressive collection of gymnastic apparatus, including a horse, a box, parallel bars, a springboard and mats. That same equipment travelled with the BBs to lots of different venues, as circumstances forced them to move many times before finally acquiring their own premises, many years later.

Normally, you could not join until you were twelve years old, but because of the date of our birthdays, some of us were allowed in a bit early. Uniforms were considerably upgraded in the BBs. Initially, you were supplied with a forage cap, a leather belt with big brass buckle cast in a BB design, and a white haversack, which was worn on parades only. Those who had been members for several years had armbands displaying the various badges they had earned, and if they had been promoted, they would have also worn stripes. Sergeants wore different hats, much like French policemen's hats. Though not enforced, the preferred clothing was a navy blue suit, white shirt and black shoes. Leather and brass work had to be kept polished, and haversacks, on parade days, had to be 'blancoed' white.

All sorts of classes became available to us; signalling, gymnastics, woodwork, ambulance, life-saving, club swinging, and national service (in wartime). I had no doubt that the gym team was the one for me, but unfortunately you were not allowed to join it during the first year, so I had to choose an alternative. I opted for signalling, which included semaphore and Morse code. Tests were held at the end of the year for certificates and badges, conducted by Captain Sinclair of the Sea Cadets at their premises in the 'Girnel' on Harbour Street. The following year I was let into the gym class.

The accommodation problem meant several moves to various premises. It is difficult to remember the order in which we moved, but after leaving North Ronaldsay Terrace just after the war, we had the use of the Town Hall, the KGS hall, an ex-navy hut opposite the Scout Hall in Willow Road, the St Magnus hall, a collection of huts on the site now occupied by the new St Magnus Centre (which had been a service canteen during the war), and the Victoria hall, now the Baptist Kirk. I think we used the King Street Kirk hall at one stage as well. Some tenancies were very short, space was limited, and of course, in most cases, we only had access to them on one evening per week.

BOYS BRIGADE c. 1945/46
Back row: Dod Newlands; Jim Dick; Malcolm Gray; Ian Argo; Bill Budge; Self; Jim Sinclair; Jack Donaldson; Ian Gray; Syd Watson; Jim Couper
Behind middle row: Bruce Wylie; _____ _____; Maurice Gray; Peter Burgess; Bob Rosie; Jim Robertson; Jim Stout; Arnold Robertson; John Foulis (Capt); Jim Muir
Middle row: _____ _____; Ian Sinclair; Arthur Flett; Evan MacGillivray; George Stout; John Flett; Gordon Rorie; Charlie Cowie
Behind front row: Gerald Moodie; Eric Moodie
Front row: Andrew Muir; Philip Stout; Billy MacGillivray; Tommy Walker; Eddie Yule.

By far the best place we had was the canteen alongside the St Magnus hall, which was bought in 1945. Unfortunately, at the time we did not acquire the site. It had everything we needed. There was a large hall for assembly, drill and gymnastics, plus a large kitchen and several smaller ante-rooms which were used for classes and officers' meetings. We also had sole use of the premises, which was used most evenings for various classes, band practices, and as a social club on Saturdays.

The social club was a great success. There had been a club in the old North Ronaldsay Terrace premises, but it was for BBs only, catering for boxing, gymnastics and other games and sports. We also held the occasional film show in the hut on Willow Road, where we were allowed to bring a partner. The new club, however, was more like a 'disco' for boys and girls from twelve up to about seventeen, where we paid our entry fee and then danced from 7-11pm. Lemonade was on sale if you were thirsty. There was always one officer there to keep things in order, not that there was ever any sign of trouble. Music was provided by Charlie Cowie, along with various voluntary helpers. Charlie was perched in a small, elevated cubicle, complete with a record player, which was attached to two loud speakers. He selected the dances and put on the appropriate music. We did Eva Three Steps, Military Two Steps, Valetta waltzes, St Bernard's waltzes, Pride of Erin waltzes, Strip the Willows, Eightsome Reels, Polkas, Quick Steps, Modern Waltzes and many others.

We also had an annual 'box social'. This was something of a mixed blessing but was intended to be an icebreaker, getting everyone involved and enjoying themselves. The drill was that each girl brought a box of food and goodies, which was handed in at the door. During the evening the boxes were auctioned. When your bid was successful, you not only got the box, but a partner to share it with. It was 'pot luck', unless someone tipped you the wink, or you got a signal from a particular girl. Mostly you took what you got. Sometimes you were in luck and got a girl you really liked or even fancied, whose Mum was an excellent baker and who did not have

Box (anti) social

KIRKWALL ATHLETIC CLUB – Gym Team 1952 (spin off from B.B. gym class)
On bars: Self; Hugh Macgillivray; Dave Keldie with son Alan; Tommy Walker; Kenny Wards
On floor: Jim Chalmers; Brian Smith

much of an appetite. On the other hand, you could get lumbered with one that ate like a horse, had a face to match, and whose Mother was a lousy cook as well. I don't suppose it was all that wonderful for the girls either.

It was a real gap in our lives when the club closed. We were in these premises for about five years, and it was a severe blow when we were told by the Kirk Session that the huts had to be pulled down to make room for a new Cathedral Manse. They were as good as their word; the huts were dismantled and we had to move to the Victoria hall. The classes struggled to keep going, with limited space and time, and of course, the social club folded. This affected a lot of kids in the town, as the club was open to virtually all boys and girls. The manse, of course, was never built, and the ground lay more or less derelict until the new St Magnus Centre opened. It is good to see the BBs still going strong, however; now totally independent with their own place.

We were particularly lucky in the officers we had. Under the captaincy of John Foulis, there was Syd Watson, Dave Keldie, Jocky Sinclair, Bill Sim, Dave Rendall, Bob Tullock, Jim Logie, Angus Findlater and others. Some of them were newly demobbed after the war, and before long they had us all marching like little soldiers, something that was a great boon when in later years we were ourselves called up to do National Service. They were popular with the lads and the Brigade prospered for many years under them.

The gym class was a good choice for me. Dave Keldie, who took it, was totally dedicated. In fact, he was dedicated to youth sports generally, and spent every spare hour he had coaching gymnastics, athletics, weight lifting and swimming. The gym team blossomed under his teaching, specialising in box work, parallel bars and human 'pyramid' building. He was a strict disciplinarian, but fair, and many young Orcadians owe him a lot. He organised gymnastic displays on a regular basis. We performed in the hall on BB occasions, in the Garrison Theatre at Hatston, Holm village, Shapinsay and Rousay; also at County and Dounby Shows, on the Market Green in front of the Cathedral and many other places. This involved transporting our equipment with us wherever we went, which was no small job.

One occasion that comes to mind because it was a bit different was when we were putting on a show for the residents of the County Home in Kirkwall. It was a beautiful, still summer's evening, and the residents and staff were all gathered outside at the front of the building. It had to take place early, too early perhaps, as most of us had just finished our tea. The show seemed to be going well, with muted applause after each performance. At one point, a member of the team, Ian, was mid-way through his speciality, the forward rolls on the parallel bars. Suddenly, with his posterior pointing straight up at the sky, he broke wind - not gently, something that may have passed unnoticed, but spectacularly, a full-blooded 'rasper', that rang round the grounds like a thunder clap. A deathly silence followed while the spectators tried to grasp the significance of what had happened, but only for a few seconds and then they erupted into a mixture of unrestrained laughter and applause. Needless to say, it was the highlight of the show, which was just as well as we were left totally incapable of following it with anything that could have compared. Even Dave had difficulty in hiding his 'delight', but afterwards we were warned severely that this was not to become a regular feature of the show. We took his warning to heart.

The BB band, previously a bugle band which had changed to pipes and drums, held considerable fascination for all the boys. You could learn the bagpipes, which entailed many hours of practice on the chanter under the tuition of Jim Couper, progressing to playing the chanter with one drone, and finally, up to three drones, by which time you were ready for the band. You were also taught how to look after your pipes; changing reeds, and keeping the bag soft and flexible by massaging it with a specially prepared mixture of honey and lanolin. Then there were the kettledrums, rarely more than three in the band, which were taught variously by Syd Cooper and Bill Sim. The option I preferred was the tenor drum, normally only two in the band, where the accent was on stick swinging rather than beating the drum. Finally, there was the 'big' drum, only one, and the big drummer was responsible for keeping the beat right. All drummers had to keep the woodwork and brass on their drums polished and the white ropes 'blancoed' for parades.

Being the 'drum major' was considered to be a great honour as you led the whole parade, swinging the mace in a variety of ways intended to add to the show. You also controlled the stopping and starting of the band. On the one occasion that I had this honour, I was in the middle of my routine when I caught the top of the mace, shaped like an anchor, in my left nostril, and from then on, led the parade with blood running all over my white shirt and best suit. That, and the subsequent rollicking I got from Captain Foulis, convinced me never to take it again. The training on the different instruments was generally good, however, and many of the lads continued into the Kirkwall City Pipe Band after leaving the Brigade.

Boys' Brigade camps were the highlight of the year. The first camp to be held after the war was in 1945, in a newly vacated army camp at Kirbister, in Orphir, near to where the water pumping station is now. We slept in army camp beds, under army blankets, and were fed by two army cooks seconded from another camp, but we did have to take turns at peeling the spuds. Waulkmill beach was no distance away and we had access to a field where we spent hours playing football. We also attended the local church on Sunday, considerably boosting the congregation and the hymn singing. I still remember the sermon that was given, not because of the content, I am sorry to say, but for the way it was delivered. The resident minister had a slight speech impediment which caused him to say 'sh, instead of 's', and the words went something like this. 'A man built hish oush on the shandsh, and the windsh came and the shtromsh came, and the oush fell.' With about 50 or 60 young lads all sitting tittering in the pews, it must have made his job that bit more of a challenge. The camp, in fact, was used all the time the schools were shut that summer by the various girls' and boys' youth organisations in Orkney. Often we overlapped, and generally we had a great time.

The following year we camped under canvas, the best kind of camp there is. We pitched our bell tents, and the marquee where we ate and assembled from time to time, alongside Swanbister beach. Our first chore was to march up to Swanbister farm where the farmer, Mr Bichan, gave us access to his *chaffy* store in the barn, from which we filled our *palliasses*. Complete with our newly-stuffed mattresses, we marched back to camp and arranged our beds, feet to the pole, heads to the canvas, six to a tent. Ex-army blankets were issued and we settled in very comfortably. The 'latrine' was a pole suspended over a trench, surrounded by a canvas 'wall', and situated in the middle of a field about 200 yards from camp. It was not much fun tramping out there at about two o'clock in the morning, in the dark, particularly on one occasion when a highland cow stuck its horny head in through the door. Thoughts of 'Old Nick' were still running through my head, as I legged it, bare-foot, breeks half up, through thistles and cow pats for the safety of the camp. From then on I managed to wait until daylight.

Unwelcome visitor

The Wick Girl Guides joined us for the second week, camping almost alongside us, and for the rest of that week the officers of both groups had their work cut out to keep order. During the night, tents mysteriously collapsed on a regular basis, followed by lots of shouting and chasing around. All sorts of other mayhem was thought up on both sides, making great entertainment for both lots - unless you were an officer.

The weather was mostly good, but on one 'typical' Orkney summer's night, all hands were called out to rescue the marquee, which was in danger of blowing into the sea. We hung on to guy ropes for grim death, not always with feet on the ground, until finally, after several hours, we succeeded in making it secure again.

On one occasion we played the local football team and I think we won. Other great attractions were the beach and the old pier along the road, which was in a poor state of repair. Between the two places we spent hours in the water. Billy Smith persuaded me on one occasion, just after midnight, to slip out of our tent dressed only in swimming trunks and run the mile or so over to the pier and back again. We then went straight into the sea and splashed around for about fifteen minutes, after which we went for another run before finally creeping back into the tent, absolutely glowing. We never seemed to feel cold. On the second Sunday there, the officers' wives and other dignitaries joined us for a 'drum-head' service. Without question it was the best camp I was ever at.

The third camp, in 1948 - there was none in 1947 - was a bit different. Arrangements were made for us to spend two weeks at the YMCA hostel in Market Street, Aberdeen. Parents were expected to pay so much towards the cost, but where that was not possible, Captain Foulis, and, I believe, at least one other officer, made up the difference. Holiday clothes were also quietly provided where necessary. We left Kirkwall pier on the *St Magnus* at 5pm, for many of us the first time out of Orkney, and sailed all night to Aberdeen. We had bunks and hammocks to sleep on, but few of us slept a wink - we were too excited - spending most of the night up on deck. Of all the many, many, times I have crossed the Pentland Firth or sailed down the North Sea, I have never seen the water so calm. There was not a ripple to be seen, and the small fishing boats that we passed were mirrored beautifully in the sea. It could have been, and usually is, so different.

On arrival at Aberdeen, we were most impressed with the sheer scale of the docks and the many large ships berthed there. After what seemed an age of manoeuvring, we were tied up at the dockside. We disembarked and marched the short distance to the hostel, and sorted out our beds. Meals were provided daily in the Bon Accord Hotel. We had various organised trips; to Duthie Park, Hazelhead Park, and to the Tivoli, where we saw Francie and Josie. The indoor swimming pool was probably the most exciting thing for a lot of us. Never having been in, or even seen, one, it was an amazing experience, and we spent many hours and a good deal of our spending money there. We went by bus to Stonehaven where the band was detailed to put on a show for the locals. Unfortunately, Jack Donaldson, our 'drum major', got a bit carried away and forgot to stop the band playing. Thankfully, after repeating the same tune about fifteen times, instead of the normal twice, Jim Couper, in the front row, indicated frantically to Ian Argo, the big drummer, to beat the stop signal. The pipers, not surprisingly, were absolutely shattered.

B.B. BAND - 1948 - DUTHIE PARK, ABERDEEN
Back row: Ian Leslie; Arnot Flett; George Stout; Ian Gray; David Robertson
Middle row: John Foulis (capt); Charlie Cowie; Jimmy Firth; Jimmy Sclater; Jim Robertson;
Jim Couper (instructor)
Front row: Jack Sinclair; Self; Ian Argo; Jack Donaldson; Bernard Borwick; Philip Stout

There were other treats laid on, but we also had a remarkable amount of freedom to roam the streets at will, as long as we reported back for meals. Some got lost of course, and though we were advised as to what number of bus to catch, no one thought to tell us on which side of the street we should be to get one going in the right direction. Fixed stops were also a new thing, and we were somewhat put out when our bus drove straight past us after we had signalled it to stop. That was rude! They would not have done that back home. It was a different kind of camp, our first view of 'city life' and a whole new experience for most of us. It was also quite an undertaking for the officers who organised it and accompanied us there.

One other outing I remember was a day trip to Westray where we had a great day visiting Noltland Castle, playing games, listening to the band and being fed by the ladies from the village at Pierowall. I formed the opinion then that Westray was almost as bonny and as nice as Shapinsay. One amazing feat was performed by Dod Newlands when he ate 11 hard-boiled eggs at one sitting. He was a big lad.

The training and discipline learned in the Lifeboys (now Anchor Boys) and Boys' Brigade were, and still are, invaluable to young lads, and it is good that they are still going strong. Having just recently attended a display night of the Anchor Boys and Boys' Brigade to watch my grandson, it was particularly pleasing to me to see that they still do a lot of the things we did; drill, competitive games, club swinging and so on. I know from my own experience that it was all excellent training, and we would have been much worse off without them.

Change . . .

Have there been any changes in my lifetime? A neighbour and good friend once said to me: 'Changes - ah yes, I could think of thousands of them over the years - but improvements, that's a different story - I could probably count them on one hand.'

Whatever your view, it would be pointless to try and list the many changes that have occurred; changes in lifestyle, the home, education, health care, attitudes, entertainment, and so on, and it was never the purpose of this book to make comparisons. For older generations they are there for all to see, and for younger people it would not be of much interest. In any case, most of them have crept up on us almost unnoticed, and the enormous difference in life 50 or 60 years ago has only really become apparent to me during the writing of this book. We are not living with a war on our doorstep any more, affecting every aspect of our lives. That in itself makes a huge difference. Let it suffice, however, to make a few small indications.

Street changes have already been mentioned, but street lighting is something that still surprises me - from the total blackout we grew up with and got accustomed to during the war, to what is almost daylight all day and night, even in mid-winter.

We did learn a lot from the war. It changed our way of living - for a time at least. It introduced us to a large influx of people, men and women, with different backgrounds, speaking different dialects, even different languages. We learned to be wary of strangers yet still friendly. We became able to cope with strange, even scary, events such as air raids, ships being sunk or damaged, planes crashing or being shot down, fleet visits, huge military parades, massive building programmes including military bases and camps - over 30 around Scapa alone - four aerodromes, air raid shelters, new roads, including the Churchill Barriers. We learned to accept changes, shortages and restrictions. For many it meant seeing relatives go away, and for some losing someone close. We learned to carry on as normal, taking everything in our stride.

In the home, features that were rare or unknown in our young days are now common in most houses, including central heating, insulation and double-glazing, with electric light and power on tap at every convenient point. There are gas and electric appliances, such as cookers, washing machines, tumble dryers, dishwashers, fridges and freezers, along with luxuries like telephones, hi-fis, stereos, compact disc players, Gameboys, and, the most powerful influences of all, televisions and computers. Mind you, a power cut 50 years ago involved nothing more than lighting a candle or lamp and then waiting until the light came back on. Now you have to spend the best part of an hour re-setting clocks and timers, and checking the contents of the fridge and freezer. Cars have also become essential to most families.

Food and eating habits have changed a great deal. Instead of eating what was mostly home-produced and home-cooked, we can buy frozen food, instant food, foreign food, such as Chinese, Indian, Italian, Mexican or Thai, produced in take-away forms, and all widely eaten now. The advent of cookers, fan ovens, deep fat fryers, steamers and, most of all, microwave ovens, have totally changed what is done in the kitchen. The preparation and clearing away of meals are no longer a major part of the daily routine. Ready meals, bought off supermarket shelves, can be heated in seconds, and for many families, with Mums who work full time, this has become a way of life. Dishwashers clean up and the whole procedure can be over in less than an hour. Eating out is a regular event for many, but not from the contents of a 'piece' tin. Even fish and chips have gone up-market, and are eaten out of a small box designed for the job, not a paper *poke*. (There was something about eating fish and chips out of a long, cone-shaped paper bag - finishing off with the small crumbly bits at the bottom.) The range of sweets is added to almost by the day, and things like popcorn, fruit and nuts of every kind, chewing gum, which contributes to the waterproofing of our pavements in the vicinity of most schools, are everyday treats.

'Loos', private and public, have featured frequently throughout the chapters, and it would not be right to ignore the developments in this area. No longer do we have to share the space with neighbours, *tatties, neeps,* coal or livestock; nor are we subject to assaults by high seas, burning newspapers, or belligerent poultry. Simple things like toilet rolls have all but rendered *The Press and Journal* obsolete, and the technology of the loo itself has advanced considerably, something that can add its own bit of excitement to a dull day. On a recent holiday we came across one that had an arm and sponge arrangement that shot out and grabbed the seat as soon as you stood up, the seat then revolved ensuring that it was thoroughly washed all round and ready for the next customer. Another, in France, had a concealed brush, which shot up when the flush was operated. It was essential that you were on your feet by this time, for it seemed bent on cleaning everything it could reach. They have certainly come a long way since the *East Hoose,* the one at Shapinsay pier, or a bucket hidden in some outhouse.

On a more serious note, a child leaving home has always been a bit of a heart-rending experience for all concerned. Going away at the fairly tender age of 17 or 18 is no picnic, and growing up fast is essential if they are going to cope with college, university or city life in general. There are more opportunities here now, with the Orkney College and the various distance learning courses available, but most young people still have to leave the islands to further their education, and as the employment opportunities here for people with degrees or other formal qualifications are still limited, most of them do not come back. Commuting is common on mainland Britain, but from Orkney it is not really an option. Quality employment to cater for all our children will always be a problem in Orkney, but at least they do not have to leave school now at fourteen, taking a job just to help with the family budget. Scapa has been both a Godsend and a curse over the years. It brought a lot of grief during the war, but it has been a major source of employment for a long time, as a naval base, an oil terminal and, hopefully, in the years ahead, as a container port.

On the subject of education, the availability of special schools for the less able or handicapped children is a great step forward. The wonderful work done at St Colm's cannot be over-stated, and had such a facility been available when we were young it would have saved many a heartbreak for parents who had to let their child go away from Orkney to get the special attention required.

Communications have certainly become more sophisticated. I can remember when the fountain pen was a huge breakthrough. If we were lucky enough to possess one we flaunted it in much the same way as we do mobile phones now. Telephone calls, made only when essential, used to involve a walk or a cycle ride to the nearest kiosk, armed with a rarely used number and a supply of suitable coins. Now calls can be made from anywhere by anyone from the age of seven upwards, on telephones carried in schoolbags, handbags or pockets, which offer text or voice communication and even send pictures. Many are also capable of linking up to the internet.

Expanding well beyond regular visits from relatives, tourism is a big thing now. This may have something to do with the fact that we live in a very unsettled world, and there is a basic human need to 'belong' somewhere - to have 'roots'. People come from all over the world, some to see relatives that they have only heard about in the 'old country'; others just to see somewhere new. They don't always appreciate what they find, cursing the weather, and the lack of this and that, but it is also a fact that many of them come back. Driving on Orkney roads can catch them out at times, particularly in the country areas where it is not only important to know that there is a vehicle coming, but also who is driving it. One irate visitor, in a hired car, tried in vain to overtake a bus, all the way from Deerness to Kirkwall, but each time he made his move, the bus tended to move into the middle of the road. On stopping at Broad Street, the bus driver was confronted by a very angry, red-faced gentleman, who expostulated; 'Do you realise I have been trying to get past you all the way from Deerness.' 'You'll jist hiv to git a faster car,' was the advice offered.

For children, the serious things in life have never been the most important preoccupation. Leisure activities are what matter and certainly there are a lot more facilities available now. No longer are they dependent on *the Openings* or *the Basin* or even the sea for swimming. The leisure centre has replaced the pier, the Peedie Sea, the *Willows,* the *East Hoose*, the old whaler and, to a large extent, some beaches. Street games are no longer possible and sledging limited. Toys have become much more sophisticated and plentiful, but many children are still as happy playing with the carton that contained the toy as the toy itself. It is amazing what they can produce with a pair of scissors, some glue or tape and an empty carton.

Holidays are so different now; Shapinsay is no longer the holiday haven for my family that it was for me. There were eight houses and farms owned by relatives that we went to on a regular basis, and we were always made most welcome. None of them is in our family any more, and the only relation I have left on the island is my cousin Isobel, who thankfully has forgiven me for leaving her in the *ipery* ditch. Had she been the kind of person to bear a grudge, I would not be able to go there at all.

Holidays as we knew them, in the country or on an island, or a farm, are still available and still enjoyable, but they are not the same. They still offer that relationship with animals and nature, however, which is invaluable for young people. It helps to create an awareness of what life is really about, instils a sense of responsibility and the necessity of caring for something. But farms are no longer what they were; something that all farmers will be delighted about. In general, they are much larger, with farmers buying up additional land to make their businesses viable. Horses have gone, replaced by tractors and powered machinery, catering for every aspect of farm work. There are no *stooks* or stacks to be built, just bales covered in black plastic. There is less hay, and oil seed rape has come to the fore. Hens are fewer, wells have run dry, and new 'occupations' have replaced much of what we did. There are still middens and you can yet find *iper* if you look hard enough, but slurry has become the big thing, something that we are all acutely aware of in spring, whether we live on a farm or not. Farm buildings have become more functional and less 'play orientated'. Farmhouses have progressed, along with town houses, with proper toilets, complete with *snibs* on the door, toilet rolls, and they are guaranteed *clucker* free. They have bathroom facilities, to make sure we have no excuse for *honking* the way we used to. Holidays have changed, and, let's face it, the sea around Portugal is warmer; not necessarily cleaner, but definitely warmer.

Travel, which at one time for the average Orcadian was almost non-existent, is commonplace now. For us, Stromness could have been (I didn't say should have been) on the moon. We did go to Dounby, Holm, or one of the islands for holidays, but that was about as far as we got. Sometimes it was necessary to move *Sooth*, or even emigrate just to find work, but to travel abroad, to places we had only heard of in the geography class for a holiday was not really an option. Places that people emigrated to in the 1930s and 40s, mainly by necessity, such as Australia, United States, New Zealand and Canada, often expecting never to see Orkney again, are familiar visiting places to many of us now. Family holidays are considered in locations like Thailand, Brazil, Cuba, Hawaii, even the Arctic Circle. Many families have 'second homes', or 'time-share' accommodation, in foreign countries, kept simply for holidays.

Every generation has had to accept change - new ideas, the disappearance of traditional ways of doing things and the introduction of new technologies. In another 50 or 60 years someone will write a similar book, perhaps one of my grandchildren, Hollie or Oliver. I wonder what they will say?

Life is certainly much more complex now and lived at a faster pace, but I think the one factor that has probably made the last few generations find things harder to accept, is the speed of change, particularly over the past 10-15 years. The explosion in electronic technology and communication systems has almost overwhelmed some people, something that affects the young as well as the more mature, as they have to keep up or someone is waiting to step into their job. By the time we have caught up with one new innovation, it has been superseded by another. No chance of a restful retirement for us; it's 'get the computer switched on and see what's on the Net'.

In the end, life has to be taken as it comes, warts and all, and we have to accept responsibility for what we do, as it will have an effect on future generations. The grass has always been greener on the other side of the fence and it is normal to look back and remember the good times and forget the bad. All I can say is that my childhood was something I recall, mostly, with great pleasure and satisfaction, and when you look at what is happening throughout the world today, you cannot ask for more than that.

Life as we knew it can never return, and most of us would not want it - not all of it anyhow. We have to be grateful for the many improvements that have been made, to appreciate that change is an essential part of life, and enjoy it. Let's face it, there are no cattle running through the streets now.

Epilogue . . .

Wherever you come from, childhood should be a wonderful time; no responsibilities, no worries; a carefree time to explore and to dream; a time to learn from experience and the people around you. This is not always possible - something few of us were aware of as kids. The world outside Orkney, even Kirkwall, did not exist for us.

Looking back I can honestly say it was mostly great, but, like all good things, it had to finish sometime. For me it ended on October 1, 1947, when Mr Leask, our headmaster, came into Miss Miller's class and told me I was needed at home; my uncle was outside, and he would tell me about it. He didn't, but I knew anyway. It was growing up time.

Appendix . . .

Then (c. 1940)	Now
Bridge St, east:	
Crawford's café	Focus on Orkney
Ballentyne's tea rooms	Torvhaug Inn
James Flett & Sons general store	Several small shops plus International Take-away
R. Garden's general store	Only Tod's bakery left
R Slater's wines and spirits shop	Orkney Photographic
Chalmers' Hairdresser	House
Turfus shoe shop	Dunfermline Building Society
Nicol Spence, ship's chandler	Energy Efficiency Centre
Sinclair's music shop	Sheila Fleet, jeweller
Albert Maxwell's grocer shop	Frozen Food Centre
Leonards	Orkney Opportunities Centre
Bridge St, west:	
Scott's fish shop	The Harbour Fry
Leitch's flowers, fruit and vegetable shop	Eastern Spice Indian Restaurant
John Foulis' butcher shop	CJ Paterson
G Arthur's bakery	Eccles Insurance Services
John Scott and Miller's	Same but much bigger
John Jolly, coal and shipping agent	Still a shipping agent
Co-op	Business Equipment Services
Co-op butcher	Rails Bookmaker
Buddy Miller, barber shop	Eric Kemp
Bob Garden's electrical shop	Eric Kemp
Albert St, east:	
Stevenson's paper shop	Owned by Leonards
Thora Jolly, hairdresser	House
Commercial Bank/Macrae & Robertson	Hydro Electric shop
Hepworth's clothes shop	Ortak
John T Flett's butcher shop	Abbey National
Zanre's café	Trenabies café
Garden's drapery	John Sclater, men's wear
Bank of Scotland	Alliance and Leicester
Peter Shearer, tailor	St Olaf's Stores
Kemp's drapers	Same
Foubister's grocer shop	Little Island
Hourston's jewellers	Same
Leith's butcher shop	Closed
Dundee Equitable	Same
Groundwater's bakery	Same
LAM Robertson, toys etc	Grooves, The Orcadian Bookshop
Morgan's jewellery and sports shop	Pat's, ladies' wear
Bank of Scotland	Same
Gorn's	Same
Lipton's grocer shop	We Frame It
Albert St, west:	
George Rendall's drapers	Leonards
Pomona café	Same
Muir's flowers, fruit and veg shop	Glue's flower shop
Cumming and Spence	Closed 2003
P C Flett's hardware and lemonade factory	Part of Cumming and Spence
Sclater's ladies' shop	Mackays
Education Office	The Stables, Solveig
Drever and Heddle, solicitors	Woolworths
Customs	Same
Orkney Herald Office	Scholes, accountants

'The Shore' and roond aboot

Smith's bakery	Shorelines Gallery
Shearer's coal office	Nimms sweet shop
JJ Smith's clothes shop	Launderama
Albert Kinema	Boots the Chemist
Wright's chemist shop	Gorn Sport
Macdonald's butcher shop	Christine Clarke, gift shop
Nicolson's bakery	The Tree Shop
Swanson's hairdresser	Hazel's hairdresser
Dr McLeod's surgery	Klaize, clothes shop
Stewart and Heddle's chemist shop	Ridgway Travel

Broad St, east:

Foubister and Bain	Same
Buchanan, lawyer	Tourist Office
Black's wool shop	Housing
Spence's paper shop	Owned by Leonards

Broad St, west:

WT Sinclair's, clothes shop	Trustees Savings Bank
Peace and Low's clothes shop	Clydesdale Bank
J Kemp's jewellery shop	The Longship
Bill Brough, watchmaker	The Longship
Kirkness and Gorie's grocer shop	The Longship
Jim Tait, cabinet maker	Orkney Television Enterprise
Post Office	Café and Community Centre
Town Hall	Same
JW Tait, grocer and hardware shop	Judith Glue
Dod Newlands, butcher shop	Judith Glue
George Bain, painter and decorator	Florabunda and MP's/MEP's Offices
Cosy Café (later)	The Orkney Museum
Billo Wick's barber shop	The Orkney Museum
Tankerness House	The Orkney Museum
Mrs Wilson's clothes shop	The Orkney Museum
National Bank	Royal Bank of Scotland

Victoria St, east:

Donny Chalmers, chip shop	R Finn, knitwear etc
Irvine's shoe Shop	Victoria Gospel Hall
Post Office.	Victoria Salon
The Royal Hotel	The Orkney Hotel
Croy's ladies' clothes shop	Vacant
Heddle's bakery	House
Geish Linklater, grocer shop	Health Information Centre
Hercus, watchmaker	The Mustard Seed café
Victoria Hall	Baptist Church
Jocky Sinclair, barber shop	House

Victoria St, west:

Dr Emslie's surgery	House
The Orcadian Office	Arch Henderson
Leask's grocer shop	Care and Repair
Mainland's Lodging house	Housing
Scott's shoe shop	Same
Zena Bain's grocer shop	House
WHB Sutherland, chemist shop	Same but bigger
Walls, fruit and vegetable shop	Part of WHB Sutherland
Dolcie Swanney, grocer shop	Zandra's
LAM Robertson – toys etc	House
Mair's fish shop	Empty
Croy's men's clothes shop	Same, but much bigger
SS Taylor, grocer shop	Calluna Fashions
Swanney's off licence	Bruce's Stores
Dad Kemp's barber shop	House

Mrs Inkster's grocer shop	House
Wm. Shearer's grocer and hardware shop	Same but bigger
Tom Brass's grocer shop	Gone

Main St:

Allan's sweet shop	House
Mary Moodie's grocer shop	House
Costie's Pavilion	Same, but no tennis courts or putting.
Roman Catholic Kirk	Same

Junction Rd, east:

Miller's radio shop	Wireless Museum
Tullock's cycle shop	Petmania
Pat Sutherland, electrical & plumbing	Closed
Garden's Weaving	Croy's, furniture
Orkney Herald printworks	House
Peace's woodyard	Post Office
Cosmo Ballroom	Peace's car showroom
Nicolson's Garage	Tullock's Garage
Gasworks	Castleyards Housing
Power Station	Car park
Johnston, vet	Same
Snack Bar	Empire Chinese Restaurant
Mackay's furniture shop	Several small businesses

Junction Rd, west:

Cattle sheds	New housing/offices
West House, toilets	New housing/offices
Miller's cycle shop	New housing/offices
Leonard's cycle shop	New housing/offices
Mackay and Wallace's Garage	New restaurant coming
Peace's woodyard	Jewson's
Mellis's Garage	The Auld Motor Hoose
Baikie's woodyard	Jewson's
J Linklater, electrician	Jewson's
CT Stewart, grocer shop	Office and flats
Robbie Milne's furniture shop	Age Concern
Auction Mart	New Library, open 2003
Police Station	Gone
J & W Tait's garage	Training Support/ Verdandi Hair Studio/ Second hand book shop
Dept of Agriculture Office	National Farmers' Union
W Firth's grocer shop	Gone
Heddle's Hatchery	Empty
Somerville Square	British Legion Club
Slaughter House	Scout Hall and Hyperbaric Chamber
Crafty	Car Park and Phoenix Cinema (closed)
McHollan's grocer shop	House
Post Office sorting office	Houses
JC Dowell, monumental sculptor	Same

Miscellaneous:

Ritchie's grocer shop (Shore St)	House
Muir's grocer shop	Part of Focus on Orkney
Garrioch, saddler	Private garage
Bill Reid's wholesale beers, etc	Gone
Grant's grocer shop (St Cath. Place)	House
Cutt's grocer shop (St Cath. Place)	Computer shop
Bella Gray's sweet shop (Garden St)	House
Jolly's coal stores	Part of Williamson's/ Orkney Delivery Services
Garden's Lemonade factory	Williamson's
Bessie Scott, grocer, (just past Cromwell Cres.)	House built on site
Cook's Laundry (Bridge St Wynd)	House
Salvation Army Hall (Bridge St Wynd)	Store
Tom Macgillivray's shoe shop (Queen St)	Empty
Knowles' wholesale fruit, etc (King St)	Empty
Craigie and Inkster, cabinet makers (King St)	Empty
Brass's grocer shop (King St)	Gone
Rocky shop (School Place)	House
Sinclair's photography (School Place)	Empty hut
Aggie Petrie's grocer shop (Bignold Pk Rd)	Gone
Leslie's grocer shop (The Willows)	Rendall's
Stout's grocer shop (White St)	House
S Groundwater, grocer shop	Bobby Hall's
JS Flett, cabinet maker (Clay Loan)	Gone
D Irvine, joiner (Clay Loan)	Gone
Glaitness Laundry (Glaitness Rd)	Empty
Alfie Wall's Cycle shop and coal yard	Shearer's car showroom and garage
Tullock's garage (Burnmouth Rd)	Peace's bus garage
Scarth's engineering (Burnmouth Rd)	Fusion nightclub
Maxwell's boatyard (Burnmouth Rd)	Scarthcentre
Meil's fish store (Burnmouth Rd)	Fusion nightclub
Drever, builder	Part of Jewson's
Toc H (Gt Western Rd)	Car Park
A Tait (Gt Western Rd)	Dental centre
Leslie, coachbuilder	Ian Swanney, car showroom
Orkney Builders	Peedie Market, now moved
Shearer's coal store (West Castle St)	Same
Davie Laughton's smithy	Additional coal store
Croy's garage (George St)	Closed
D Kirkness, chair maker (Palace Rd)	McLennan's Toymaster
Library	Unknown future
Porky Horne's butcher shop	B.Clark, optician
Mrs Allan's sweet shop	Part of B Clark
Linklater, dentist (Watergate)	House
Down, dentist (East Rd)	House

Glossary . . .

A'	All
Aboot	About
Appro	Approval
Ba'	Local game played in the streets with a hard ball
Back chat	Talking back or arguing
Bawled out	Told off
Bands	Straw bands for tying sheaves
Basin, the	Kirkwall harbour
Bed sek	Mattress or bed sack
Ben	Best room
Bere bannock	Scone made from bere (a type of barley) meal
Brecks	Slopes or humps
Brandies	Sticklebacks
Breeks	Trousers
Brig, the	Corner at Stevenson's paper shop
Bunk	Bed
Burn, the	Willow burn
But	Living room
Bye	Over
Chaff	Oat husks
Chaffy house	Part of mill where husks were collected
Chanty	Chamber pot
Claes	Clothes
Clapshot	Potatoes and turnips mashed together
Cleg	Horsefly
Click	Girlfriend or boyfriend
Clicking	Snatching
Clipe	1. Tawse; 2. Tell-tale
Clootie dumpling	Large fruit pudding boiled in a cloth
Clucker	Broody hen
Cogs	School toilets
Comfy	Comfortable
Comper	Monkfish
Cookie	Sweet bun
Coorse	Coarse or rough
Coorse biscuit	Large hard biscuit
Corny	Cornslip
Cossie	Swim suit
Covers	Blankets
Crabbit, Crabby	Bad-tempered
Craigs	Crags
Cuithes	Coalfish
Curly Dodie	Wild pink clover
Dead man's plunge	Stone breaking water with no splash
Digs	Lodgings
Dippers	Swimming trunks
Drooned	Drowned
Dross	Coal dust
Dungarees	Overalls
Dunter	Eider duck
Dux	Top pupil in school.
Eastie	East Road
Ebb meat	Cockles, whelks, etc, found on the beach.

Erse	Posterior
Ersy crab	Hermit crab
Euchre	Card game
Fanners	Machine for dressing oats
Feesked	Mildewed
Filler	Funnel
Gan	Going
Gansy	Jersey
Giblets	Gizzard, neck, etc, of a hen.
Gillick	Quarter bottle or gill
Gouster	Shout
Greet	Cry
Grimlings	Twilight
Grottie buckie	Cowrie shell
Gruelly belkies	Porridge eaters
Hid	Had
Had	Hold
Halfie	Half bottle
Hamnavoe	Stromness
Hiding	Thrashing
Home brew	Home-brewed ale
Honking	Smelling
Hookeries	Sliding in the squat position
Hookers	Squat position
Hoo's	How is
Hoose	House
Howdie	Midwife
Iper	Midden ooze
Jersey	Jumper
Keek	Kick
Kirn	Churn
Kirn milk	Milk left in churn after making butter
Longs	Long trousers
Luk	Look
Lugget	Clip on ear
Mallies	Marbles
Min	Man
Mither wit	Mother's wisdom
Neb	Beak
Neeps	Turnips
Nippit	Tight
Ooo	Wool
Osted	Ostoft
Palliasse	Mattress
Partans	Crabs
Patty	Small flat cake
Patty supper	Patty and chips
Peedie	Small
Pee-hee	Toady
Peevers	Hopscotch
Picco	Tag
Pig	China hot water bottle
Place	Farm
Plantings	Woods
Plimmies	Plimsolls
Plook	Pimple
Plushney	Catapult
Poke	Paper bag
Pooties	Small cod

Protectors	Metal studs
Pud	Dessert or pudding
Pund	Pound
Quartie	Quarter bottle
Rattin tail	Wild plant shaped like a rat's tail.
Scaffie	Street sweeper
Scarman's head	Sea urchin
Scooties	Starlings
Scruttling	Scratching
Scullery	Kitchen
Sharn	Cow dung
Shepherd's reed	Mouth organ
Shin	Climb
Sillock	Coalfish
Simmet	Vest
Sitten	With chick embryo inside.
Skelp	Smack
Skin	Play truant
Skitherie	Stone skimming over surface of water
Skitter	Excreta
Slock	Extinguish
Sluice	Water course
Smookan	Spraying
Snib	Door catch
Sooans	Fermented oat flour
Soorick	Sorrel
Sooth	Mainland Scotland and/or England
Spoots	1. Razor fish 2. Gutters or rones
Stirling	Starling
Stook	Bundle of six sheaves set up to dry
Strap	Tawse
Straps	Braces
Street, the	Includes Albert Street, Bridge Street, Broad Street and Victoria Street.
Tatties	Potatoes
Teeick	Lapwing
Tell-pie	Tell-tale
Thunderbox	Toilet
Tinklers	Travelling people
Took	Tuck
Toon, the	Kirkwall
Toonies	Kirkwallians
Toorie	Knitted bonnet
Toot	Posterior
Toot-fie	Upset or confusion
Tot	Small whisky or other spirits
Traipsing	Trudging
Trump	Jewish harp
Wan	One
Wand	Fishing rod
Wap	Starting handle
Whins	Gorse
Wupped	Twisted
Yow	Ewe